# WAKE UP!
# YOU'RE ALIVE

## MD'S Prescription For Healthier Living Through Positive Thinking

## by Arnold Fox, M.D., and Barry Fox

Health Communications, Inc.
Deerfield Beach, Florida

Arnold Fox, M.D.
Barry Fox
Beverly Hills, California

Library of Congress Cataloging-in-Publication Data

Fox, Arnold, 1928-
    Wake up! You're alive / Arnold Fox and Barry Fox.
        p.        cm.
    ISBN 0-932194-66-4
    1. Health. 2 Mind and body. 3. Mental healing.
    4. Medicine.
    Psychosomatic.        I. Fox, Barry. II. Title.
    RA776.5.F695 1988                                          88-7213
    613--dc19                                                      CIP

ISBN 0-932194-66-4

Published by: Health Communications, Inc.
            3201 S.W. 15th Street
            Deerfield Beach, Florida 33442

# Acknowledgments

This is the fourth book we've written together. Even though we claim the credit, they were all family efforts. One of the advantages of being part of a big family is that there are always a lot of people around. After all the jokes and din, after all the opinions — and everyone in the Fox family is an expert in something — they all pitch in and help.

While there is one of us (AF) who loves to talk about how we can change the world, about his experiences in the Army and what it was like growing up in South Philly, there's another (BF) who keeps us on track and makes sure the writing goes smoothly. BF: "Dad's stories are great the first 17 times, then they get a little old. But there's no escaping. So we listen, amazed at how the stories keep changing over the years."

Behind the two men writing the book is a woman. But what a woman: Hannah, wife and mother. Quietly, without fanfare, she reads the pages hot off our computer, comments on the writing, goes to the printer and does all the things that have to be done. She is a perfect counterbalance to the exuberant father and the son who keeps telling the father to focus on the task at hand. When it looks like we're getting run down, she either sends us to the club to exercise, or whips out the chicken soup (making sure to skim the fat off the top, of course).

And the other members of our family:

Howard and his wife, Robin, now have three children: Melanie, Joshua and Andrew. We've got to admit, it's a real challenge to write with three kids, ages six, four and one, coming over to visit, playing with the computer and trying to tickle us while we're working. But we enjoy spending time with them, and even volunteer for more. It's this sort of atmosphere that helps build our love and affection for each other, and which we can see in the latest generation of Foxes.

By the time you read these words, Eric will have finished his Internal Medicine Residency in New York. He and Fienie, his wife, are very compassionate people who are looking forward to a great life. I'm glad medicine is going to have a new young doctor filled with joy, enthusiasm and happiness, along with skill and knowledge. We know Eric will have a special way with patients: **BF:** "He has a way of making me feel important." **AF:** "He always makes me laugh." We both feel "up" with him.

Although Steven has the no-nonsense approach of an attorney, he's filled with the milk of human kindness. **AF:** "Steve knows me the best. He recognizes better than I do when I'm down. He'll come over to play my favorite songs on the piano, encouraging me to sing along (preferably on key). Then he says: 'OK, you're feeling better. I've got to get back to law school and study'."

Barbara and her husband, Danny, bring a sense of newness to our lives. Barbara always had a way of doing that. In the Scriptures it says we should walk in the newness of life. With Barbara, we always do. **AF:** "I remember when we'd walk down the street together, when she was a little girl. People would stop us to admire the rich blue color of her eyes. She always made me feel young — she still does." **BF:** "I remember, when she was two years old, teaching her how to turn the bowl of

iv

spaghetti upside down on her head."

Bruce is the youngest, and you'd think we'd have it down pat by now. But every child is different and a joy in their own way. With him we're learning about rock concerts, railroad trains and video games and how to coach Little League baseball and soccer. (See the Apple Power story later in the book.)

**AF:** "I'm still amazed. I think how lucky I am, a boy from South Philly, who gets paid for doing something he loves to do. Namely, seeing patients as a doctor. I pinch myself to see if it's real. I think of myself as a boy from South Philly who became a country doctor in Beverly Hills. I teach people about joy and happiness, about utilizing the mind, body and spirit in combination with my medical knowledge. In return, I receive love and happiness."

# Foreword

## Norman Vincent Peale

*WAKE UP! YOU'RE ALIVE* is one of the most absorbing books I have had the pleasure of reading. It is written in a fascinating, lively, narrative style that at once picks up the interest of the reader and carries one along page after page.

But the book has a message also, a clear and defined statement that one *can* live a healthier, happier life by conditioning the thoughts that pass through the mind.

This book is written by a distinguished medical man, one recognized for his scientific training and talents. But he is aware that the statement made by an ancient scholar is very potent: "Mind is everything. We become what we think."

I must confess that I felt real good physically upon reading this book. And that feeling of well-being has remained with me through the days following. The humor with which the book is interlaced is infectious. You will find yourself laughing often. And do you know, laughing is good for you?

So, to feel better yourself, permit me to give you a prescription: Read and study *WAKE UP! YOU'RE ALIVE*.

Dr. Fox is joined in authorship by his son, Barry Fox, and they make an amazing father and son team. Together they have produced a book which I expect to be very popular.

# Contents

Dedicated to
Carlos Cueva,
the little godson I once carried,
now a Marine.

**Also by the Foxes**

*The Beverly Hills Medical Diet*
*DLPA To End Chronic Pain And Depression*
*Immune For Life*

**Norman Cousins,** adjunct professor at UCLA School of Medicine and renowned author of *Anatomy of an Illness,* congratulates the authors of *Wake Up! You're Alive* by saying, "You enable people in need of help to discover their own resources, even as they avail themselves of the best that modern medical science has to offer."

# RX: How To Read This Book

1. Begin by reading the entire book from beginning to end. Read it in one sitting if you can. If not, spread the reading out over a couple of days. When you get to the end of each chapter, be sure to follow the directions and repeat the affirmation over several times — that's very important.

2. Don't put this book up on the shelf when you have finished reading it once; once is not nearly enough. Keep the book close by you. Re-read one chapter every day. Start at the beginning and work your way through, a chapter a day. Find the time to do this: You're worth it. When you come to the end of each chapter, memorize the affirmation. Say it over and over, etch it into your memory.

   Make each new affirmation you learn a part of your daily routine. Repeat the affirmations over and over, out loud and to yourself, several times during the day. Say your affirmations morning, noon and night. When you say them, see them with your mind's eye. As it says in the Scriptures: "Day and night shall you meditate upon them." Soon these remedies for disease and distress will become second nature to you.

3. If you're feeling down, re-read the chapter that has to do with your distress. Pay special attention to the

quotes and affirmation in the chapter.

Here's my prescription for your new life, the happy, healthy and successful life you so richly deserve:

---

Prescribe For:                              Arnold Fox, M.D.
    You                                Internal Medicine
                                  Beverly Hills, CA

                                    Date: Today

RX: **Wake Up! You're Alive**
Dispense: One Book

Sig: 1. Read **Wake Up! You're Alive** all the way through.
     2. Re-read the book, one chapter every day, over and over again. Memorize the affirmations in each chapter. Make them part of your daily routine.
     3. When troubled, read the chapter relating to your distress.

□ Do not substitute                           □ Refill daily

_____
        Arnold Fox, M.D.

---

# Introduction

### ". . . Therefore, Choose Life . . ."

One Sunday night many years ago I was at home with my family when I received a telephone call from the charge nurse at a suburban Los Angeles hospital. She told me a woman was scheduled for surgery the next morning, and the neurosurgeon wanted an internal medicine specialist to make sure the patient was fit for surgery.

"I've called seven internists and none of them will come out," she said. "You're the eighth one I've called. Will you come?"

I hesitated, thinking that I didn't want to be number eight: I wanted to be number one. But I agreed to go, got in my car and drove across town to the hospital.

The charge nurse explained that an elderly woman had been brought to the hospital in a coma two days ago.

"She's in a deep coma. No one has been able to bring her out of it. The neurosurgeon has scheduled exploratory surgery early tomorrow morning."

I walked rapidly to the patient's room, the nurse following slowly behind. The heavy door slammed behind me as I went into the room to find an elderly woman lying flat in bed with her arms straight at her sides and her eyes closed. Seeing that I was alone in the room and that the door was shut, I impulsively put my mouth close to her right ear and shouted, "WAKE UP!"

The elderly woman scared the heck out of me by suddenly jumping up into a sitting position. Just then the charge nurse walked in, saw the patient sitting up in bed and screamed: "Oh my God! You cured her! It's a miracle! It's a miracle!" Before I could say a word, she ran out to tell the other nurses. In no time the room was filled with nurses come to see the great miracle awakening.

"It's not a miracle," I protested. "I just yelled, 'Wake up'." But the charge nurse wouldn't believe me: "I was right behind you, Dr. Fox. I would have heard you yell. You did something to bring her out of that coma!" (She didn't take into account the sound-proof door.)

Nothing I said dissuaded her from telling the others that I performed the impossible by bringing the elderly woman out of a coma in just an instant. Needless to say, I jumped from number eight right to number one on the Internal Medicine specialist list. The nurses insisted that I be called whenever a difficult case presented itself.

Several days passed before I discovered what had happened to the woman I had "cured". Elderly and very hard of hearing, she had felt suddenly dizzy, so she laid down in bed and closed her eyes. Just then her daughter walked in and, thinking her mother was dead or dying, called for help. Soon the old woman was in the emergency room, where needles were stuck into her spine and arms, she was probed, blood was taken out of her, medicines were injected in. There were bright lights, people running about and orders shouted. Terribly frightened by all this commotion, and not understanding what was happening, the poor woman suffered a reaction in which her mental distress was converted into the physical symptoms of a coma. The more that was done to her, the more frightened she became. And so she stayed in that state until I came along, and figuring it couldn't hurt, yelled, "Wake up!" into her ear.

Years later an international jetsetter, who was also my patient, lay unconscious in a hospital near downtown Los

Angeles. He had suffered a stroke following surgery. The doctors said he would be paralyzed on his right side.

At the request of his family I went to the Intensive Care Unit to see him. It was night, the hospital was quiet and I was alone in the room with the comatose man. Could it work twice, I wondered? I leaned over and yelled, "WAKE UP!" into his ear. He didn't jump out of bed, but he did move his arms and legs — all of them. That told me he wasn't paralyzed, as the doctors had feared. I knew he was going to get better.

I went back to the waiting room where his very large family was gathered. They were immensely relieved when I told them that I felt he would be all right. I stayed with them until two in the morning, telling them stories of patients, including the one about the elderly woman who woke from her coma. I told them about my patients who got over their illnesses once they changed their beliefs; once they got rid of their hatreds and other negative feelings; once they began to believe in themselves.

Yes, the family agreed, they knew people like that. They believed a strong spirit was vital for health, but were surprised that a medical doctor would say so, too. Finally the jetsetter's daughter said: "It's great to hear these inspirational stories from a doctor! Why don't you put them all in a book?"

"What shall I call it?" I asked.

Without hesitating she answered, "Wake up."

"Wake up, you're alive," said another relative.

This book is a look at the power of the human mind and spirit, as seen through the eyes of a physician. The case histories and stories in this book illustrate the relationship between your thoughts, beliefs, health and disease, and the lessons that are to be learned. Your mind and spirit are very powerful: You, and only you, determine whether they will be a strong medicine or a terrible scourge. I hope that reading about people who have used their inborn powers to overcome disease, adversity, poverty and other handicaps will inspire you to make the most out of your own life.

Most of us are not in a coma, like the elderly lady. But neither are we fully awake and enjoying life. We're puzzled and frightened. We feel the ground slipping away under our feet as values, morals and ethics change. We shudder to see traditional support groups melt away. We suffer the effects of personal and economic woes.

From my experience as a medical doctor I can tell you that your health absolutely depends upon your having a strong and enthusiastic spirit. I've treated thousands of patients who had no business being sick, and certainly should not have died. But they were unhappy; they felt overwhelmed by life, and they gave up living.

I've also seen many patients who lived despite terrible diseases. These were people we doctors had given up on. They had nothing on their side but an indomitable will to live. That burning desire to live actually changed the biochemistry of their body, creating conditions that destroyed their disease and restored them to health. They lived because they refused to die.

No medicine in my doctor's bag can cure people who have lost their will to live. But getting them interested in life again, making them want to live — that's a powerful medicine, one I love to administer.

As Moses said to the children of Israel:

> . . . *I have set before you life and death, blessing and cursing: therefore choose life . . .*
>
> *Deuteronomy 30:19*

You have a choice. You can choose, depression and disease. I've seen many patients do just that. Or you can choose to live life to its fullest, enjoying the health, happiness and success you so richly deserve. I urge you to choose life. Wake up! Because you're alive.

# Be You Transformed By The Renewing Of Your Mind

*He who has health has hope; and he who has hope has everything.*

*Arabian Proverb*

Most of the physicians in this country are in the wrong business. Trained to diagnose exotic diseases, prescribe medicines and perform surgery, they are ill-equipped to comfort most of the patients they see.

A bold statement? Consider this: Ninety percent or more of the people flooding doctors' offices are suffering from problems caused by loneliness, alienation, estrangement or separation from family and friends, dissatisfaction and general unhappiness.

I know of no drugs or surgeries to cure these ills. Medications and operations can relieve some of the symptoms, but they do nothing about the underlying problem, allowing it to fester and spread unchecked. To

1

make matters worse, medications and operations have innumerable side effects, some more dangerous than the original disorders.

As a nation we're physically and spiritually ill. We look to our medical system for solace, but that system does not have the solution. As a matter of fact, the average doctor hasn't even been trained to recognize the problem.

What are some of these problems? Headaches, neckaches and backaches; stomach pains, ulcers, spastic colitis and other gastrointestinal upsets; sore throats, colds, the flu and lingering infections; fatigue, sleep disturbances, irritability and anxiety, plus other vague signs and symptoms of distress.

## Tension-vascular Headaches

I've treated many patients suffering from tension-vascular headaches. Tension-vascular headaches are related to disturbances of the blood flow in the head ("vascular" refers to the system of arteries and veins).

The scenario is repeated countless times across the country every day. A worried patient goes to the doctor who, after examining him or her, solemnly pronounces the diagnosis: tension-vascular headaches. Suddenly everyone is happy. The doctor is happy because the case is wrapped up, neat and simple. The patient is happy because his pain has been validated and legitimized. Furthermore, he's given a prescription, a written "promise" that the problem will be taken care of. The pharmacy is happy because they're going to make some money filling the prescription. Even the insurance company is happy, for they have an impressive-sounding diagnosis to feed into their computer. Everyone is happy, but the poor patient still has the pain. Why? Because tension-vascular headaches are due, for the most part, to the stresses, strains and emptiness of a life devoid of fulfillment, enjoyment and laughter; of a life without love and the other emotions that make life worth living. The doctor may give you an analgesic to relieve the pain or a tranquilizer to mask some of the stress, but he can't give you what you really need: love, a feeling of belonging, perhaps some joy. All we doctors have are medicines that may or may not work, but will, in all probability, cause side effects.

## Heart Palpitations

What about palpitations of the heart; those irregular heart beats you suddenly feel, that pounding of the heart that worries you so? One of my patients often got palpitations while sitting home alone on Saturday afternoons waiting for the phone to ring. But the only call was from a recorded sales voice asking her to buy something. And a little earlier there was a wrong number. What happened to all the people she knew at work? Well, some have families, boyfriends, girlfriends — she'll see them on Monday, but tonight will be a long, lonely night. Every once in a while as she sits staring at the phone, cursing its silence, she can feel a little flutter or pounding in the upper part of her chest. A doctor has told her not to worry, it's just a slight irregularity of the heart. For insurance purposes he wrote "cardiac irregularity" on the chart. Strange. The thing that cares most about this woman's diagnosis is the insurance company's computer. Now at least, she belongs somewhere: in the computer.

One doctor said he could give her medicine: Quinidine, Procan or others. "But there's really nothing wrong with your heart," he explained.

She didn't believe that. She thought the doctor was withholding important information about her heart. So she went to another doctor, but this one scared her away because he was too anxious to prescribe drugs, lots of drugs. He laid out a detailed medication regimen, assuring her that if the drugs didn't work, surgery would.

Next on her itinerary was the "big" doctor at the university hospital. Here lots of tests were done, confirming that there was nothing physically wrong with her heart. Finally she came to me.

I repeated the appropriate tests and studied the other doctors' reports before telling her what she admitted she knew all along: there was nothing wrong with her physical heart. The problem was in her spiritual heart, which was lonely and sick. Piece by piece her spiritual heart was dying. And medicine, I added, won't help. Medicine will worsen matters. It'll become a crutch for you to lean on, an excuse for not dealing with the real problem: the loneliness. And because medicines all have side effects which require other medications, what's left of your health will soon be buried under piles of pills.

## Stomach Pain

What about stomach pain, that burning, gnawing pain in the pit of your stomach? It's not a terrible pain, but still it worries you. It doesn't seem to be related to what you eat. Oh yes, now and then when you have something spicy, it may hurt but the pain usually hits when you look back at the missed opportunities in your life, when you look at friends who seem to be leading happy lives, who have somebody's loving arms around them, who are laughing, perhaps celebrating one of their children's birthdays. Others can see the future unfolding before them in joyous anticipation, but you only see the missed opportunities and a lonely, forbidding future. You think of that and your stomach hurts.

Your "shrink" tells you that it is a lonely world, and that your stomach is the sounding board for your emotions. Yes, you've taken Tagamet to dry up the stomach acid — it helps for a while — and you've tried the new drug with the stronger dose that's supposed to work for a longer period of time. You drink the liquid antacids; you've changed your diet. You've had the upper gastrointestinal X-rays, and maybe they found a spasm of the upper GI tract, a small ulcer, duodenitis or gastritis. If your doctor was very thorough, he or she looked down into your esophagus, stomach and duodenum with a long fiber-optic instrument called an esophagogastroduodenoscope.

"Ah ha!" he smiles. "I've found an erosion, a little wearing away of a localized area of the lining of the stomach. It's a good thing we caught it so early!"

You're so happy you could kiss the doctor. He's found something physically wrong. He's proven that the pain is not just in your head. It actually makes you feel good — for a little while — to know that you have a physical problem. Doctor and patient are pleased. You've got a diagnosis to prove that your pain is real, and the doctor has proudly diagnosed another case. The insurance computer is also happy, of course, because all the blanks are neatly filled in.

Both you and the doctor know, however, that the gastric erosion was caused by stress, by your feelings of alienation, of lack of belonging, of a lack of someone to love and someone to love you, and your inability to connect with anyone or anything. You can take all of the pills the doctor gives you — and he's got a lot to prescribe. You know the pain will go away for a little while, but will soon return because that empty spot in your heart, that yearning for something, has not been filled.

## Spastic Colon

What about spastic colitis? It's a very fashionable disorder. With spastic colitis you can't be too far away from a bathroom because all of a sudden the cramps hit in the lower abdomen (belly), sending you to the bathroom with diarrhea or loose stools. And the more you have to push yourself at work, the more you realize that you chose the wrong man or woman, over and over again the more you must explain to yourself just exactly why life is so unfulfilling, the more spastic your colon becomes.

Perhaps you've found the "ideal" man this time — you know he's the one. Six weeks or six months later, however, the luster has rubbed off your relationship. Perhaps he's not what you thought he was, or maybe your desperate neediness scared him away. The cramps come back, so you open up the medicine cabinet again. Let's see, should I take the codeine this time? How about Donnatal? That seemed to work last time. Or maybe the sample of Reglan the doctor gave me? All the medicines help a little but don't really solve the problem. You ask yourself if the problem is with you or the men. Ouch! Just thinking about it sends your colon into spasm. It hurts too much to admit the truth.

## Fatigue

"So tired of dreaming of you." Doesn't that sound like the lyrics to a 1940s song? It's from "*So Tired*", a song that was popular when I was in the Army. I think of this song often as I listen to patient after patient tell me that they're so tired. They come to me with bulging folders accumulated during their journey from doctor to doctor.

Here's a patient folder containing a six-page report from the Mayo Clinic, a many-paged condensed report from the Scripps Clinic in La Jolla, several evaluations from local doctors, and even reports translated from French and Italian.

*So Tired.* Is there a physical cause? Or are you so tired because you haven't achieved what you want? That person? Job, dream or goal you set your heart on?

The medical/industrial complex thrives on fatigue. It's one of the most common complaints we doctors hear. Diagnostic centers love fatigue. It gives them lots to do; it keeps their machines busy.

"Let's see," says the specialist at a big medical university anywhere in the world as he consults your file. "Our preliminary tests fail to show a cause for your fatigue, but don't you worry. We're going to have you seen by the psychiatrist. We're going to do special tests on your brain, nervous system and sleep patterns. We'll do an electroencephalogram to measure your brain waves. We'll have your heart checked out by our cardiologist. He'll get to the heart of the matter. That's a joke. And we'll also do an echocardiogram. Let's see, a 2-D, M-mode, oh, and yes, a doppler. I'm going to check off for the cardiologist to make sure a stress treadmill test with a thallium scan is done. And we'll check your heartbeat for 24 hours with a Holter monitor. That's a little box you'll be connected to for 24 hours to record your heartbeat. If there's anything wrong with your heart, we'll find it. We'll certainly learn about your heart."

And learn about your heart they do. But there's nothing wrong with it. The cardiologist, in fact, marvels at the beauty of the "pictures" of your heart he's studying. There's nothing wrong with the physical heart that pumps blood through your body. But nobody checks your spiritual heart.

So off you go to the next specialist — the gastroenterologist. (That's a fancy name for someone who checks out the digestive tract, from the food pipe to the stomach to the intestines, and also looks up from the lower end of your intestines.) Soon you're lying on the examining table, a long tube pushed up into your bowels, listening to the doctor enthusiastically describe what he sees in you. If you're lucky, you can watch the whole thing on a monitor mounted on the wall. Please, please, you pray, find something wrong with me. Not serious, just something to explain why I'm so tired and unhappy, something they can cure easily.

The doctor turns the scope around and around, he pushes it in and out. You can feel it rumbling around inside you. "Ah ha!" he says "Here's a small, shallow erosion, a little scratch in the musoca, the lining of the large intestine. And there's also a small hemorrhoid," he remarks as he withdraws the scope. Now everybody's happy again. The doctor has identified the problem, you have a diagnosis and some pills to take, and the insurance computer has the proper words for your file: colitis and hemorrhoid.

The big medical center has investigated you from stem to stern, but somehow you know that as well-meaning, well-trained and sympathetic as these doctors are, they didn't really help you. Deep within, you sense that your problem is spiritual, not physical. The pills may be of temporary value, but you know they're not going to give you a sense of belonging or a feeling of being loved.

## Sore Throat

How about your sore throat? Is it a strep sore throat, a virus sore throat? Is there a hoarseness of the voice or any fever? What made your throat hurt? Could it be all those unhappy feelings you treasure? Those hatreds you've been nursing so carefully? Negative thoughts can't make germs appear, but they do create conditions that allow germs to flourish. What does your doctor say? More drugs and more tests?

In one sense, all those tests we doctors order are worthwhile. They help you to see that you really don't have a dread disease. And sometimes that knowledge helps you look within yourself in search of the problem — and the answer. Thank the doctors and the high-tech tests for ruling out a physical disorder, then look inside yourself for the problem — and the solution. Learn how to tap into the great power hidden deep inside of you, the power to turn your life around and put you on the road to happiness, health and success.

---

Modern medicine cannot really help the overwhelming majority of people, not when our diseases are predominantly spiritual. That's why we must look to ourselves, to our spirits and thoughts, for comfort and cure.

---

## Thought-Disease

"Come on, Dr. Fox," some have said. "You talk as if you believe there's no such thing as a real physical problem, that every disease is caused by unhappiness or poor thoughts."

There are many people suffering from "physical" disorders caused by viruses, bacteria, injuries, genetic mistakes, toxic pollution and so on. *But most of the people we doctors see in our offices and in the hospitals are the victims of "thought-disease".* Thought-diseases are illnesses caused or worsened by the unhappy thoughts that fill our heads.

Let me tell you about a 42-year-old woman who came to see me recently. She complained of diarrhea, allergies, spastic colitis, cold hands and feet, dermatitis, headaches, various minor illnesses, loss of appetite, sexual dysfunction, depression, fatigue, irritability, anger, nervousness, worrying thoughts, insomnia and nightmares. She often woke up in the middle of the night in a panic.

I took a thorough personal and medical history, performed a physical examination and called for the appropriate tests. I found a few easily treatable "physical" disorders and imbalances. But her responses to some written questions, not the regular examination, revealed the most about her. When asked to choose the statements that most closely reflected her attitudes, she selected the following:

*I am usually completely scared.*
*In life I have no goals or aims at all.*
*My personal existence is utterly meaningless, without purpose.*
*Every day is exactly the same.*
*If I could choose, I would prefer never to have been born.*
*In achieving life goals I have made no progress whatsoever.*
*My life is empty, filled only with despair.*

*If I should die today, I would feel that my life has been completely worthless.*
*In thinking of my life, I often wonder why I exist.*
*The world completely confuses me.*
*With regard to death, I am prepared and unafraid.*
*With regard to suicide, I have thought of it seriously as a way out.*
*I regard my ability to find a meaning, purpose or mission in life as practically nil.*
*Facing my daily tasks is painful and boring.*

She was also asked to finish a series of statements. The words following the dash in each sentence are hers:

More than anything, I want — *peace of mind, no more skin problems.*
My life is — *sad.*
I hope I can — *discover what is wrong with me.*
I have achieved — *nothing.*
My highest aspiration — *(no response)*
The whole purpose of my life — *is no existence.*
Death is — *peace.*
I am accomplishing — *nothing.*
To me all life is — *(no response)*
The thought of suicide — *is a way to end pain and hopelessness.*

Do you think this woman is an extreme case? She's not. The difference between her and the millions of people desperately searching for answers to their problems is only the degree to which they are unhappy, unsatisfied, unfulfilled, unable to find a reason for going on.

I can't tell you exactly which of this woman's negative attitudes "caused" this or that ailment. Nor can I say that her unhappy thoughts were solely responsible for her physical ills. But you can be sure that there is a very strong relationship between thoughts and disease, and that the drugs and surgeries we physicians offer so eagerly will not solve the problem — not the real, underlying problem.

"How can I help this woman?" I wondered, as we sat together in my office, discussing my findings. I had various medicines in the office, and the pharmacy downstairs had thousands more. But there was no pill that would make her happy, nor one to give her a reason for living or even a little hope. A quote from the Bible ran through my mind: "In vain you have used many medicines; there is no healing for you" (Jeremiah 46:11).

Finally I told her, "I can help you with some of your problems. For a real cure, however, you must rely on yourself. There's a record player in your head, and it keeps playing the same horrible record over and over, telling you that life is lousy and that you don't deserve to be happy. You've got to change that record. Put on a new record, one that's filled with belief, enthusiasm, joy, love, perseverance, optimism and forgiveness. That's the medicine that will really help you."

---

The human mind and body are one and the same, different aspects of the same whole — you. Unhappy thoughts are invariably reflected as diseases of the body. But happy thoughts encourage a healthy body. That is a basic law.

---

## Locked In And Lonely

Most of us live in big cities. From New York to Washington, D.C., from Los Angeles to San Diego, it's almost all one big city. Millions of people live together in loneliness. The day begins as we read the bad news in the paper, gulp down make-believe fruit juice and gobble up fatty foods. In the car we turn on the radio news to hear about more disasters, killings, robbings and corruption. Perhaps we listen to the radio psychologist, seeing ourselves in almost every one of the unhappy callers. Maybe it's just as well, for we have no one else to share

our problems with. And all the while we have to deal
with people cutting in front of us, with impolite and bad
drivers.

Silently we long for the time when people were
friendly. Life isn't what it used to be. Today we're afraid
to say hello to strangers and we don't dare to pick up
hitchhikers. We sit in our cars, locked in, windows up. At
home we lock the doors and pull the drapes because
prowlers like to look through the windows. The people
next door have lived there for years, but we don't know
them. We do, however, know of some people who are so
lonely, they go to the shopping mall just to be with other
people. But if they talk to anyone, they're looked upon
with suspicion: Why are they talking to me, what do they
want? Are they trying to find out where I live?

Our relationships are brief and fleeting. Before we
even find out what kind of ice cream the other person
likes, they're out of our lives. Today's relationships are as
disposable as the plastic wrap that covers our ice cream
bars. We devour the ice cream bar and throw away the
stick, just as we do with our relationships.

Go to the trendy nightspots in any city to see people
standing eight to ten deep. Watch the young men and
women, the older men and women, all longing to connect
with another human being. Instead of real contact, they
get empty conversation, words they can barely hear over
the music and crowds, the same opening lines, instant
love or instant rejection, instant sex, instant gratification,
instant desolation. They're seeking a real sense of
belonging, a meaningful relationship. What they don't
know is that every relationship is meaningful — but what
is the meaning?

We lock our doors, we lock our minds, we lock our
emotions. A 30-year-old friend of mine forgot to lock his
car door one day. When he stopped at a red light on Vine
Street in Hollywood, a man jumped into his car and put
a knife to his ribs, demanding money. My friend was
slow in responding so the anonymous assailant shoved the
knife between his ribs, puncturing his lungs and sending

him to the hospital. My friend said he had special locks on his car, but he'd forgotten to use them that one time. Since then, he's locked shut all the doors in his life, be they physical, emotional or spiritual. Who can blame him? But who can envy his locked-in life? Doctors sewed up the knife wound, but cannot mend the rent in his soul. Only he can do that.

## We Have Met The Enemy — It Is Us

Last week, a young woman whom I hadn't seen for two years came to my office, hugged me and said, "Dr. Fox, I'm so glad to see you! I feel so tired, so weak. You know, I've been in Los Angeles for four years and I still don't know anybody. I go to my job, I talk to a few people, then I go home to my little apartment. I feel so unhappy. I took your advice and went home to Nebraska. For six weeks I felt so wonderful! My aches, my pains, my headaches went away. What should I do?"

I told this woman that I felt her body was telling her something, that she felt connected at home, a member of her family with a role to play back in Nebraska.

"Am I a failure if I give up and go back home?" she asked.

I replied: "It has nothing to do with failure. You may have a better-paying job in Los Angeles, but the quality of life is not as good for you in Los Angeles. Weigh the advantages of a better-paying job against the disadvantages of loneliness and the fatigue that drags you down."

I'm not saying that Los Angeles or any other big city is necessarily bad, or that small town living is always good. This woman thrived in Nebraska because that's where her support system, her family and friends were. Her support system could just as easily have been in Philadelphia, Chicago, Minnesota or San Francisco. Geography doesn't determine whether or not you are happy. Happiness depends on you.

Let me tell about another patient of mine, a 37-year-old writer who came to my office one day and said, "Arnold, I'm tired of the rat race, the big city, the noise, the traffic and the stress. My dad's a stockbroker, my brother's a CPA. They are so stressed! Everybody in this city lives for their two-week vacation so they can get the heck out of here. I'm moving up to the mountains. I can write just as well up there. I'll be able to ski a lot, and when I'm skiing, I'm happy."

I wished him luck. Two years later — almost to the day — he called me long distance, "Arnold, I have terrible pains in the pit of my stomach. I'm coming down to see you."

A few days later he was at my office in Beverly Hills. He told me that the stomach pains were getting worse, often waking him up at night. They wouldn't go away unless he ate something or drank a glass of milk.

It sounded to me as if he had a peptic ulcer. To make sure, I gave him a thorough physical examination and performed the appropriate tests. He did indeed have an ulcer.

"How can I have an ulcer?" he asked incredulously. "I didn't get one living in Los Angeles, which is the most stressful place there is."

We spoke for a long while, and finally he admitted that living on the mountain wasn't as much fun as he thought it would be. Yes, the skiing was great, but most of the people were as unfriendly as they were anywhere else, and he still fretted about getting assignments and meeting deadlines.

"But still," he persisted, "why didn't I get an ulcer in Los Angeles?"

I explained that the problem is not geography, for wherever you go, you take yourself. And for the most part stress is not "them" or "it": Stress is "us". The problem lies within us — our thoughts, perceptions, beliefs. We can move, find a new job or spouse, change our name and get a nose job — but a negative attitude will quickly make the "new you" as unhappy and unhealthy as the old.

*But if the problem is within you, so is the solution.* It's possible to change perceptions, attitudes and beliefs, to change them for the better. And when your thoughts become positive, distress melts away.

## What Makes You Angry?

"But, Dr. Fox," many patients protest, "I don't want to have negative attitudes. Living in the big city makes me that way. And my husband (wife/children/boss/job/ neighbor) makes me angry, and with the traffic and unfriendly people, I can't help but be negative."

Wrong! Nobody *makes* you mad or *makes* you happy or *makes* you angry or *makes* you loving. People and events are only a stimulus: *You* decide to react by becoming mad, happy, angry or loving. Remember: *You* are the only one who is thinking the thoughts that fill your head. *You* are the only one who can determine what those thoughts will be, whether they will be positive or negative. That means you can begin, right now, to turn your life around.

Our world is not always a pleasant place. There's pollution, overcrowding, economic worries, crime and what-have-you. I don't have a magic wand that will turn the world into a Garden of Eden. If we can't always change the world, however, we can change our attitudes.

---

You are the only one thinking in your head. You, and only you, determine how you will react to events.

---

## I Will Put None Of These Diseases Upon Thee . . .

In most cases we bring disease upon ourselves. My experience with patients over the past 30 years has been that the overwhelming majority of patients unknowingly cause and/or contribute to their own physical and emotional ailments. They don't know that every negative thought they entertain is as dangerous as a physical germ. Every negative thought they think harms their health, shakes their peace of mind, disrupts their love life and personal relationships, and contributes to their failure at school, work and life in general.

But every positive thought encourages happiness, health, loving relationships and success in all aspects of your life. That's why I want you to learn how to fill your mind with the most positive thoughts possible, the kind of thoughts that will make your life as rewarding and fulfilling as you long for it to be — as you deserve for it to be.

---

The best medicine isn't in a bottle — it's in your head.

---

## Spiritual Transfusion

A few months ago a very beautiful 40-year-old woman came to see me. She was so striking, in fact, that another patient asked me if she was a model. No, I told him, she was a registered nurse coming to interview me to see if I should be her physician. Now, I think it's a good idea for patients to interview doctors, looking for one whose health philosophy suits their own. This goes along with my idea that people should take an active role in their health and become their doctor's partner, rather than a passive receptacle for prescription drugs and poorly-digested medical jargon.

This woman spent about 30 minutes throwing questions at me, asking how I would approach various diseases. Then to my surprise she said: "Dr. Fox, your answers are very simplistic. They keep coming back to the way you think, plus what you eat, exercise and your environment. Don't you think that's too simplistic an approach?"

I thought about this for a moment, then replied: "My approach is simple, not simplistic. Simple answers work the best. The very complex answers — drugs, surgeries and so on — are not doing the job. In many cases they compound the problem."

"I'm glad you stuck to your guns, Dr. Fox," she smiled. "My experience as a registered nurse in the Intensive Care Unit has convinced me that the simple answers are the better ones."

Here's one of the simplest and most effective remedies to the plague of negative thinking now afflicting us: a spiritual transfusion. A blood transfusion brings new life to your body by filling you with healthy red blood cells, the white blood cells that fight disease, nutrients and more good things. A spiritual transfusion brings new life to your body and mind by filling you with the positive thoughts that straighten out your body chemistry, by striking down disease and depression and promoting health, happiness and success.

I want you to picture yourself lying on a bed with a transfusion bottle hanging up on the wall. The bottle is filled with positive thoughts: belief, enthusiasm, love, happiness and so on. Imagine a tube running from the bottle into your right arm: All the good thoughts from the bottle are running through the tube and into your arm as you give yourself a spiritual transfusion.

With this spiritual transfusion, you replace every hateful thought in your head with a loving thought; each gloomy thought with a happy thought; every weak thought with a strong thought; thoughts of disease with thoughts of health; all negative thoughts with positive thoughts. As you imagine yourself receiving a transfusion of spirit, I want you to say, to yourself:

*I am happily transfusing myself with the most positive of feelings.*

*I am joyfully replacing hateful thoughts with loving thoughts. I am enthusiastically replacing gloomy thoughts with happy thoughts. I am rapidly replacing weak thoughts with strong thoughts. I am happily replacing thoughts of disease with thoughts of health. I am eagerly replacing every negative thought in my head with a positive thought, knowing the result will be a healthier, happier and more successful me.*

This spiritual transformation is what this book is all about. Forty million Americans are depressed. Thirty-five million are tortured by arthritis. Thirty million women battle Premenstrual Syndrome. Twenty million of us are plagued by fatigue, listlessness and lack of energy. Twenty million more have high blood pressure, and another twenty million suffer from tension-vascular headaches. Fifteen million are tormented by lower back pain. Millions more have irritable colons, peptic ulcer disease, heart irregularities, diabetes, sleep disorders and other problems. The list goes on and on. All these people — and more — will benefit greatly from a powerful spiritual transfusion.

In the coming chapters we'll be looking at different emotions and attitudes. We'll see how some help us, while others hurt. You'll learn how to take advantage of the helpful attitudes. Soon you'll master the use of spiritual transfusion of positive thinking. You'll sweep dangerous negative thoughts from your head and replace them with the happy, loving, accepting, enthusiastic thoughts that promote physical and spiritual health, happiness and success in your life.

## Be You Transformed

There are five cardinal virtues everyone must embrace if they are to enjoy health and success in life:

enthusiasm
belief
love
forgiveness
perseverance.

These are your sword and shield, the beacons lighting your way through life. The next five chapters are devoted to these cardinal virtues. Read each one carefully and memorize the affirmation at the end of each chapter. It's these affirmations that make the spiritual transformation possible. Religiously take the steps necessary to make each of the five virtues a part of your words, thoughts, habits, actions and beliefs. Give yourself a spiritual transfusion of the five virtues. Be you transformed to health, happiness and success.

# Enthusiasm, Endorphins And The "E-Spot"

*None are so old as those who have outlived enthusiasm.*

*Henry David Thoreau*

For many years I was privileged to have as a patient a wonderful lady who taught me that boundless enthusiasm is a kind of magical elixir of health and longevity. Ruth was 85 when I first met her, but she had a youngster's enthusiasm for life, finding joy in most everything she did. At the age of 101 she was still brimming with health, happiness, humor, strength and vitality. Her vision was crystal clear, her hearing sharp and her skin supple.

Every year Ruth's daughter brought her to my office for a checkup. The daughter, Naomi, looked and felt all of her 60 plus years. The routine never varied. I would examine Ruth and find her to be in good health and spirits. Naomi then would cantankerously insist that I instruct her mother not to fast all day on a certain religious holiday. Ruth would smile patiently, then explain, "Dr. Fox, I've fasted every year since I was 13.

Do you really think it's going to hurt me to fast again?" I'd have to say no, fasting for one day would not hurt her, as long as she drank water.

I once asked Ruth what it was like to be old. She grinned as she said: "I haven't the faintest idea because I'm not old. Ask my daughter. She's older than I am."

"How can your daughter be older than you?"

"Look at her. I love her dearly, but she's an old cuss. I'm healthier and livelier than she is. I'm younger than she is."

"What's your secret?" I inquired.

"Getting as much fun out of life as children do from playing. Pure fun. On my 75th birthday I was sad because I thought I was old. Thank God, that only lasted a minute. I've been young and happy ever since. I don't know how many years I have left, but I look forward to every day with enthusiasm."

## Entheos = In God

Enthusiasm: What a magic word! I feel chills down my spine just thinking about enthusiasm. Enthusiasm is that special something that revs up the engine of life, kicks your spirit into high gear and says "Get out there and live!" Enthusiasm is the sparkle in your eyes that makes everything seem extra bright and shiny. Enthusiasm is the bounce in your step, the bright smile on your face and the joy in your heart. Enthusiasm is love and inspiration. Enthusiasm is all that and more.

Let's take a quick look in the dictionary. "Enthusiasm" comes to us from the Greeks, to whom "entheos" meant "in God". What does "in God" mean? It means to be inspired by God. And since God is love, being enthusiastic means being inspired by love: love of an idea, love of a person, love of life.

I believe that the full definition of enthusiasm includes a feeling of ardor, a word which comes from the Latin for "to burn". Enthusiasm, then, is a glowing, fiery-hot passion, zeal and eagerness. You know the feeling. It's like the tingling when you're on your way to see that someone special. It feels great, doesn't it? You feel as if you can overcome any obstacle, walk on walls, conquer dragons, do anything you want. Now imagine feeling that feeling of enthusiasm every day, all day long. Wouldn't that be great? You bet!

---

To be enthusiastic is to be "entheos", full of God. Since God is love, to be enthusiastic is to be full of love for life.

---

## Rejoice And Be Glad

*Walk in the newness of life.*

*Romans 6:4*

Ruth said that her secret for healthy and happy longevity was getting as much fun out of life as children do from playing. Children are full of enthusiasm. To them, most everything seems new and wonderful. As adults we tend to become bored by life, jaded and cynical. We forget how to be enthusiastic as we focus in on the unpleasant parts of life.

Let's take a lesson from Ruth. She knew how to see the world with the enthusiastic eyes of a child. That's not to say she was childish. Just the contrary, she displayed a great deal of wisdom and maturity. But she never forgot as she went through life how to be delighted and enthused by things both common and rare. As you'll learn a little later, enthusiasm and other positive thoughts actually help prevent disease and tilt the scales in favor of youth and vitality. That's why we should all walk in the newness of life.

---

Walking enthusiastically in the newness of life tilts your biochemical scales in favor of health and happiness.

---

## The Enthusiastic Mind

I once asked Ruth to complete a series of sentences, the same ones as the unhappy 42-year-old woman with the laundry list of complaints I described in the previous chapter. The difference in their outlook on life is as clear as day and night. (The words following the dash are Ruth's.)

More than anything, I want — *to continue living as I have.*

My life is — *a gift from God.*

I have achieved — *happiness, health and love.*

My highest aspiration — *is to teach my great-great-grandchildren that the secret to life is waking up each morning enthusiastically.*

The whole purpose in life — *is to thank God for giving me life by loving the life he gave me. Every minute of it.*

Death is — *a long way away, I hope!*

I am accomplishing — *I am happy every day.*

To me all life is — *a blessing.*

The thought of suicide — *never thought of it.*

## How Enthusiastic Are You?

Are you enthusiastic? Take these two short tests to see. First, complete the sentences, any way you like:

1. More than anything, I want —
2. My life is —
3. I hope I can —
4. I have achieved —
5. My highest aspiration —
6. My whole purpose in life —
7. Death is —
8. I am accomplishing —
9. To me all life is —
10. The thought of suicide —

Each of the next nine sentences has two possible endings. Circle the number that best describes where you stand between the two endings.

---

1. Each new morning is:
a great new start.                                                                a drag.

   10    9    8    7    6    5    4    3    2    1

2. Obstacles are:
challenges to overcome.                        the reason I'm such a failure.

   10    9    8    7    6    5    4    3    2    1

3. My friends:
enrich my life.                        are no big deal, but you have to talk to someone.

   10    9    8    7    6    5    4    3    2    1

4. If I were to die right now:
many people would be sad.                        no one would notice.

   10    9    8    7    6    5    4    3    2    1

5. If it were up to me, I'd:
live ten lives like the one I have now.                        never have been born.

   10    9    8    7    6    5    4    3    2    1

6. Setbacks are:
temporary problems.                                                    my lot in life.

   10    9    8    7    6    5    4    3    2    1

7. Most of the time I'm:
interested and enthusiastic.                        bored and unenthusiastic.

   10    9    8    7    6    5    4    3    2    1

8. My personal relationships are:
joyful, wonderful.                                        miserable failures.

   10    9    8    7    6    5    4    3    2    1

9. Life is:
great!                                        a never-ending source of pain.

   10    9    8    7    6    5    4    3    2    1

---

Compare your answers to the first set of sentences to Ruth's highly enthusiastic responses and to the depressed woman's. To whom are you closer? As for the second set of sentences, the higher your numbers, the better. I like to see my patients average eight or more, with no scores below seven.

## Profile Of Enthusiasm

The enthusiastic person wants all the good feelings, relationships and successes they already have — and more.

The enthusiastic person shouts out that life is good, enjoyable and worthwhile, a blessing and a treasure.

The enthusiastic person longs to continue living life to the fullest, and looks forward to sharing life's joy with their loved ones.

The enthusiastic person feels that they have achieved good things, and looks forward to accomplishing more.

The enthusiastic person finds meaning and purpose in life.

To the enthusiastic person, death is something that happens a long time from now; it's a natural event not to be concerned with. And suicide? That's something an enthusiastic person never thinks about.

The enthusiastic person faces life with cheerful optimism and confidence, for life is a joyful journey through a delightful and sometimes surprising world, a trip enjoyed most when shared with others.

The enthusiastic person sees love everywhere, waiting to be shared.

The enthusiastic person is always looking forward, always has lots of things they can't wait to do.

Where others curse, the enthusiastic person laughs it off. When others cry, the enthusiastic person finds joy. While others admit defeat, the enthusiastic person redoubles their effort, for they have confidence in their ability to succeed.

The enthusiastic person is easy to recognize: They're the ones walking in the newness of life.

## The Man Who Wouldn't Die

I'm spending so much time describing the enthusiastic person because enthusiasm is the first of the five cardinal virtues, a powerful one upon which the others are built. Memorize the features of enthusiastic persons; the way they walk, talk and act; model your life on theirs. Here's an inspiring case history illustrating the tremendous power of enthusiasm. I call it "The Man Who Wouldn't Die."

I met this incredibly wealthy man, whom I'll call Frank, many years ago when he lived in a giant Beverly Hills mansion attended by many servants. A tennis court and an Olympic-size swimming pool sat in the back garden next to the guest house. An entire wall of his study was filled with stereo gadgetry.

"Do you know how to use all this stuff?" I asked.

"No," he said, grinning. "I'm tone-deaf. But I love pushing the buttons!"

Every weekend Frank threw a lavish two-day party for the movie stars, jet-setters and politicians he palled around with. Back when I first met him in the early 1960s, he was spending more for one of these parties than I earned in a year. I went to some of those parties: the food, the liquor, the servants, the gifts he handed out — amazing, and amazingly expensive.

Then one day it was all gone. All of a sudden Frank found out that his partners had been embezzling money from the business. In no time at all he lost his house, cars, servants, pool, stocks and bonds, vacation home, jewelry, paintings, stereos, wife and friends. His partners went to jail, and Frank wound up living in a one-room apartment over a garage in a seedy part of town.

What an incredible blow! Not only had he lost his
wealth and possessions, but his wife and friends all
disappeared.

"Not one of them was willing to help me out," he told
me as we sat in my office.

I had just examined him and after hearing the whole
sad story, didn't know how to tell him he had another
cross to bear: diabetes. His kidneys were shot, his
circulation was poor, his heart was suffering and his
vision fading. All the high living, coupled with his failure
to heed the warning signs, had finally caught up with
him. Frank was wiped out, all alone and in very poor
health. His prospects for regaining his fortune were poor,
for even though he was innocent of any embezzling or
other wrongdoing, people felt he was tainted by associa-
tion. They wanted nothing to do with him.

Men have killed themselves for less than this, but to
Frank it was all past history. "I've always been an
enthusiastic kind of guy, Kid." (He always called me
"Kid," even though he was only ten years older than me.)

"Ever since I was little, I've bounced out of bed in the
morning raring to go. I always felt as if I had something
important to do today and couldn't wait to do it. That
enthusiasm made me a millionaire because I didn't have
anything else going for me. No education, no connections, no seed money, nothing. Strictly enthusiasm. The
day I knew my money was definitely gone was the same
day my wife left. I went to bed thinking I'd never be
enthusiastic again, but the next morning I bounced out of
bed feeling that I had something to do and I couldn't wait
to do it, just like always. I knew exactly what I had to do:
Earn it all back, every penny. I'm going to do it, Kid. I
started with nothing but enthusiasm and I've still got it, so
it ain't over yet!"

"It's great to see you so enthusiastic," I said. But to
myself I added, "You haven't got long to live. The
diabetes is too far advanced."

This was long before modern kidney dialysis machines
and other therapies were available. Even if they were, I

doubt whether they would have made much of a difference. The disease had attacked too many parts of his body. You could tell he was in trouble just by looking at his enormously swollen legs and feet, filled with fluid his heart was unable to pump through the body. I gave Frank the medications and treatment of the day and hoped for the best.

To my delight, Frank made liars of my pessimistic predictions by taking generous amounts of that powerful medicine called enthusiasm. I don't know how he did it, I don't know where his battered body found the strength to go on.

"I love the challenge, Kid, the chance to do it all over again," he said. "How many people get that chance?"

Frank firmly believed he would make a second fortune solely on the strength of his enthusiasm. You know what? He did it. It took a long time, but he did it.

Frank measured his success in terms of dollars earned and business deals consummated. I read the fascinating story of his success in his medical file. What an inspiring story the file told! Page after page describing a body that simply refused to quit, despite that battering inflicted by the diabetes. As months passed I said to myself that he should be in bed. As years passed I said he should be dead, but Frank refused to let the devastating illness slow him down. Every time he came to my office in the years that followed, he was more enthusiastic and spiritually alive than ever.

"I've got something to do today, Kid," he'd say. "I can't wait to do it!"

All things must finally go the way of all flesh, of course. Frank's incredible enthusiasm gave him many extra years, but his body finally fell before the onslaught of diabetes. Frank died rich in dollars. More importantly, he lived rich in enthusiasm, joy and spirit.

I've treated thousands of patients suffering from diabetes in all of its manifestations. I know too well how it can destroy the kidneys, heart, circulation, limbs, sight and hearing. I've read the progress of this scourge in too

many a patients' chart. I can tell you that Frank had no
business living as long as he did. With 30 years of
experience in the "front lines" of crisis medicine under
my belt, I firmly believe that Frank's enthusiasm was
chiefly responsible for his astonishing achievement and
remarkable longevity.

Enthusiasm can make a difference in your life, too!

---

Of all the weapons in the physician's armory, none are as
mighty as enthusiasm.

---

## The "E-Spot": Where Enthusiasm Begets Endorphins

How does enthusiasm turn disease into health, despair
into joy and failure into success? By acting on the "E-
spot" in your brain.

The human brain is like a house that's been added on to
and remodeled several times. What was once a little
shack is now a great mansion. Your "E-spot" is located
where the new brain — the cerebral cortex — meets the
old brain — the limbic system. Here, in structures buried
deep within the brain, thoughts are converted into
biochemical and electrical messengers, then shipped out
to the body to spread the news.

Throughout your life the "E-spot" converts good
thoughts like enthusiasm into endorphin hormones and
other beneficial messengers of health and happiness. I
call it the "E-spot" because I've singled out enthusiasm
and endorphins and the outstanding examples of cause
and effect. So when I talk about enthusiasm and
endorphins, remember that they represent whole classes
of thoughts and substances.

## Endorphins, The "Morphine Within"

What are endorphins? They're a group of recently discovered hormones that block chronic pain, elevate the mood and enhance the immune system. How much would you pay for a substance that can do all that, better and faster than any drug known to man? Luckily, your lifetime supply of endorphins is absolutely free, for your body produces these precious hormones on its own.

In one of our previous books, *DLPA To End Chronic Pain And Depression* (Long Shadow Books, 1985), Barry and I showed how the endorphins — beta-endorphins, dynorphin and the others — can block even the excruciating pain of cancer and childbirth. We also explained how raising the levels of endorphins and other biochemicals in the body can lift the terrible veil of depression. Since *DLPA* was written, new studies have been reported, describing how the endorphins work with the immune system, strengthening your built-in Department of Defense in the fight against disease.

But here's something everyone should know: Your thoughts, your good enthusiastic thoughts, can turn the endorphin faucet wide open!

## You Can Literally Think Your Way To Health

We've known for years that happy enthusiastic people tend to fare better than the dour types who find "joy" in unhappiness, although we could never tell you exactly why. That changed when a 1981 study at the University of Tennessee Center for Health Sciences showed that thoughts, and thoughts alone, can increase endorphin levels in the body.

Endorphin levels were measured in the spinal fluid of 32 patients suffering from chronic pain. Then doctors gave the patients placebos, "sugar pills" with no medicinal value. Placebos work by somehow converting a person's belief in the placebo (however misguided) into

biochemical changes in the body that mimic the supposed action of the placebo. In other words, the patient's
positive thoughts ("I'm going to get better") are somehow
made a physical reality.

Fourteen of the patients (slightly over 40%) felt better
after taking the placebo. That was expected, for placebos
are effective in 30% to 40% of patients.

*The amazing part was that endorphin levels rose in all
14 patients who reported pain relief.* Here at last was an
explanation for the placebo effect: Positive thoughts
raised endorphin levels, and in turn endorphins blocked
the pain.

Those 14 people literally "thought" their endorphins
up. Their belief in the placebo, their enthusiastic
anticipation of pain relief and all their other good
thoughts, were converted into endorphins (and possibly
other beneficial substances). Their thoughts tipped their
biochemical scales in favor of health. You can do the
same, using your "E-spot" as a fountain of endorphins
and other beneficial substances.

---

Every thought you think goes toward the making of your
body chemistry.

---

## The Endorphin Response To Enthusiasm

You already know how to use your "E-spot", and you
do so often, although you may not be aware of it. I gave
this demonstration to a young patient who doubted the
existence of this critical part of the brain.

"What makes you feel good?" I asked.

"Seeing my boyfriend," she promptly replied.

"Would you feel good if he were here in this room, and, oh, you were sitting in his lap?"

"Yes," she said, a big smile brightening her face.

"You're smiling. How come?"

She looked a little surprised. "I . . . I feel good."

"I know. You had a big smile, your eyes lit up, your posture changed. What made that happen? Not your boyfriend, because he's not here. *Thinking about him* made it happen. Your happy thoughts became the endorphins and other substances that put the smile on your face, the sparkle in your eye and a chill up and down your spine. Those same substances also gave your immune system a boost, although you couldn't feel it. It all happened in less than a second, just because you thought good thoughts."

"Is this similar to making your heart beat faster and feeling sick to the stomach by thinking scary thoughts?"

"The exact same idea. Thoughts change body chemistry. Scary thoughts, angry thoughts or hateful thoughts prompt the 'fight or flight' response to stress. Positive thoughts, enthusiastic, happy, cheerful and exciting thoughts trigger the 'endorphin response to enthusiasm'. The two responses are opposite sides of the same coin."

It all happens in the "E-spot", that part of the brain where thoughts and notions are translated into chemical and electrical messengers that create the physical sensations we associate with feelings and emotions. This means that you have within you a powerful tool for health and happiness. Use it freely.

---

The endorphin response to enthusiasm allows you to trigger the release of endorphins and other good substances that in the right amounts can turn your life around for the better.

---

## Diagnosis: Anenthusiasma

What happens to those who, for one reason or another, rarely touch their "E-spot"?

Jane Welch was a 40-year-old woman I met while participating in a church seminar in Redondo Beach, a beautiful coastal city south of Los Angeles. After the speeches and discussions were over, Jane pulled me aside to say that she hadn't felt well for years.

"Mostly I'm tired. And my neck aches constantly. Not too badly, but constantly. Can I come to your office?"

A few weeks later she came to see me as a patient, bringing with her a thick stack of photocopied medical reports. "It saves time to photocopy the reports and bring them to the new doctor, instead of waiting for you to send for all of them," she explained.

"How many doctors have you been to see?" I asked.

"You're number fifteen. The others couldn't find anything wrong, but I know I've got something. I want you to find it."

"If the other doctors couldn't find anything . . ." I began to say, but she cut me off.

"I'm not a hypochondriac, Dr. Fox. Before this happened, I hardly ever saw doctors, and I never took medicines unless it was absolutely necessary. I'm not a complainer, but I'm not crazy either. There is something wrong with me. Physically. You've got to find it."

I took Jane's personal and family medical history, performed a thorough physical examination and called for the appropriate tests. A week later we met again to discuss my findings.

"Let's begin by looking at what's right with you," I said. "Your individual organs — heart, lungs, liver, etcetera — are very easy to check. They're all in good shape. Your brain is a good one, and the neurological examination is normal. These other doctors agree," I said, tapping the pile of photocopied reports.

"Then what do I have? It's got to be something. I'll go to a hundred doctors if I have to to figure this out!" she declared, setting her jaw with determination.

"You're suffering from anenthusiasma," I said very seriously, coining the word right on the spot.

"What's that? Is it serious?"

"It can be a deadly disease. But we can control it, even reverse it with the right treatment."

She looked very worried. "What is it?"

"Anenthusiasma. 'An' from the Greek for 'not, without'. 'Enthoes,' from the Greek for 'in God, full of God, full of love'."

"Go on," she instructed eagerly.

"In other words, you are suffering from a lack of enthusiasm; enthusiasm for life, for yourself, for someone else, for a project, for an idea. The only thing that seems to get you excited is proving that you have a dread disease. Let me read you some of your answers to the Purpose In Life test you took. You wrote:

More than anything, I want — *not sure.*
My life is — *all right, I suppose.*
I hope I can — *not sure.*
I have achieved — *nothing special.*
My highest aspiration — *not sure.*
My whole purpose in life — *is there a purpose?*
Death is — *part of the scheme of life, no big deal.*
I am accomplishing — *as much as anyone else, I suppose.*
To me all life is — *life is life, that's what it is.*
The thought of suicide — *maybe for some people suicide is all right, if they're really sick or very unhappy. Most people, however, should stick it out.*

"Life is no big deal to you, it's a big blah. Am I right?" She nodded slowly. "What makes you happy?" I asked.

She thought for several seconds before replying, with an indifferent shrug: "I'm as happy as anyone else. I'm not depressed," she added hastily, defensively.

"No, you're not depressed. You're *un*impressed. Unimpressed with yourself, with your job, your family, your friends, unimpressed with all of life. That's what

anenthusiasma means. That's why you're tired all the time
and your neck hurts.

"Don't go to any more doctors, you've been to enough.
Instead, get some enthusiasm in your life, that'll take care
of your problems! Act enthusiastically, walk enthusiastically, talk enthusiastically, behave enthusiastically. Get
your endorphins flowing, that's what they're there for.
God, I feel enthusiastic just talking about it!"

"But *I* don't feel enthusiastic," she objected. For every
one of my suggestions on how to get enthusiasm she had
a "but" . . . "But I don't feel that way . . . but I don't
think it will work . . . but I must have a physical problem . . .
but my job is lousy . . . but my husband's a jerk . . .
but . . . but . . . but . . ."

Gently but firmly deflecting her "but's", I insisted that
she learn to rev up her enthusiasm and stimulate her "E-
spot" regularly. It took a while, but she finally agreed to
try. A month later she reported that her neck pains were
"mostly gone" and she had "much more energy".

"I didn't believe it would work, but I began feeling
better right away. Not a lot at first, but enough to keep
me going. I'm glad I stuck to it, because now I feel much
better."

---

Anenthusiasma — the absence of enthusiasm — can be a
terrible disease. Treat it now, with the only sure cure: generous
doses of enthusiasm.

---

## Making Yourself Enthusiastic

Is it possible to *make* yourself enthusiastic? You bet it
is! And it all begins when you act enthusiastically.

Years ago I was asked to consult on the case of a 27-
year-old man from the hill country near the Russian-

Turkish border. "For centuries my people were fierce and independent warriors. Now we are slaves to the Communists," he said disgustedly when we first met. "I came to America to be free again."

Unfortunately this man, call him Peter, found it difficult to build a life for himself in big-city Los Angeles. Lacking both a higher education and a good command of English, he found himself working as a poorly-paid laborer. Friends were few, although he managed to find a girlfriend. Like Pete, she was a lonely Russian immigrant. Not having much money didn't bother him, for he was accustomed to being poor. But being alone was hard for this man, who was used to sharing life with a large family and friends.

One day, while lifting heavy crates at work, he felt something snap in his back. He couldn't lift anymore and was soon fired from his job. Not long after that his girlfriend broke off their relationship. Not angrily, not because he was a bad guy. She just wanted to move on, try her luck elsewhere. So this descendent of proud mountain tribesmen found himself alone, injured, unemployed and broke in the big city.

He began suffering from severe diarrhea, cramps and shooting pains in the stomach, rapidly losing weight, strength and spirit. When told he had severe colitis, he got even worse. Notice that he got worse when *told* he had colitis. That bad news was converted to bad biochemistry, making him even sicker. By the time I saw this once husky, 6 foot 2 inch man, his weight had plummeted from 180 pounds to 105. He was in serious trouble, flat on his back in the hospital.

I examined him thoroughly, repeating all the tests and then some. I pushed a flexible scope down his esophagus to check his stomach, and a different scope up the other end to examine his colon. I ran blood tests, special X-rays, the works. But I knew the real problem lay in his spirit, not his gastrointestinal tract.

"I wanted to be proud of myself, like an American," he sadly told me, his voice barely a whisper. "I wanted my family back in Russia to be proud of me for becoming an American. Am I going to die here with no one to care?"

I don't know what hit me, but suddenly I found myself standing at the head of his bed, pointing at him and exclaiming: "You can be proud! You can be a proud American, and you can make your family proud of you!"

"What?" was his very surprised reply.

"How do Americans act?" I asked, not realizing that I was shouting at him.

"Americans are proud," he answered in his weak voice.

"What are they proud of?"

"Their country."

"Are you proud of this country?"

"Yes," he answered, his voice a bit stronger, more alive.

"Then sit up and say it!" He struggled into a sitting position in bed. "Say I'm proud of America!"

"I'm proud of America."

"Louder!"

"I'm proud of America!"

"Smile when you say that!"

For the first time, I saw him smile. I saw a little sparkle in his eye, I saw him strengthen his back as he exclaimed: "I'm proud of America!"

"And I'm going to get better so I can become a citizen!" I prompted him.

"Yes," he said excitedly, voice strong. "I have to get better so I can become a citizen. I *have* to get better!"

That's when I realized I had been shouting at a bedridden, very sick hospital patient. I looked around rather sheepishly, wondering if anyone was watching from the hall, or if George M. Cohan was about to march in singing *Yankee Doodle Dandy*.

But Peter didn't care if anyone was watching. He was trying to get out of bed, saying, "I have to get a new job to be a citizen."

Wow! I had never seen enthusiasm work that fast before. It took effect so rapidly because Peter had a strong goal already in place: to be a proud American citizen. His enthusiasm fed into that goal, zoomed right to his "E-spot" and turned on the endorphins and other beneficial substances that in the right amounts promote health, happiness and energy.

## "Assume A Virtue"

Peter became instantly enthusiastic by acting enthusiastic. No, I take that back. He couldn't *act* enthusiastic because he was sick in bed, with needles stuck into his arms. All he did was to *think* enthusiastically. His thoughts, his *good* thoughts, were enough to begin the healing process.

Your emotions may not listen to reasoned arguments, but they jump to respond to physical or mental activity. So "assume the virtue," as Shakespeare said. Assume the virtue of enthusiasm. Wrap it around your shoulders and hold it tight. Don't worry if it feels uncomfortable at first, like a borrowed coat. Assume the virtue with faith and determination. It'll soon feel very comfortable.

Peter assumed the virtue of enthusiasm — enthusiastically! He stuck with it as his "E-spot" acted on that great desire of his to become a proud American. All the depressing thoughts that had caused the illness in the first place, the "I won't make it", the "life is too hard", the "I'm a failure" and the rest were swept aside by wave after wave of "I'm going to do it!" His body chemistry quickly realigned itself as he regained his weight, health and spirit.

---

Assume the virtue of enthusiasm. Walk enthusiastically, talk enthusiastically, think enthusiastically and act enthusiastically. In no time at all you'll *be* enthusiastic.

---

## Make Enthusiasm Your Business

"I agree with what you say about enthusiasm," a middle-aged man suffering from cancer said to me. "But how can I be enthusiastic in the face of my serious cancer? All the doctors have told me there's no hope. Except you."

I told this man about a woman I was asked to see not very long ago. Her name was Donna Reed. You probably remember *The Donna Reed Show* that was popular on television back in the 1950s. It's still playing on the cable channels. I still love to watch it.

Unfortunately, I only got to know this brave woman in the last months of her life, as her struggle against cancer came to a sad end. We sat in my office on the seventh floor of a building in Beverly Hills one day, and she pointed out of the window to her house, and told me about her family, her career, her dreams. It was easy to see that she had a zest for living and a good supply of enthusiasm, despite her terrible illness. She told me that she grew up on a farm in the midwest during the Depression years. Times were tough, especially for her parents, who battled to keep both farm and family together. The hours were long, the labor was hard and the prospects were dim. But her farmer-father had faith and enthusiasm. He gave her those two virtues, which are probably the most precious gift a parent can give their child. Donna told me that she renewed her enthusiasm regularly, in good times and bad. It was a powerful tool in her life, she said, and it affected the people around her for the better.

A little enthusiasm goes a long way. Your "E-spot" can turn even a tiny drop of enthusiasm into the biochemical substances that put a spring into your step and sharpen your outlook on life. So make it your business to be enthusiastic, no matter how good or bad life seems to you at the moment. Odds are we're all going to live through booming economies and depressions, wars and times of peace, national ups and downs, as well as personal ups and downs. Such is the nature of life. Whatever your state today, make it your business to be enthusiastic.

---

Enthusiasm is more precious than gold or silver, status, power or possessions. Without enthusiasm, all your gold is worthless rock, your power a chore and your possessions uninteresting. It's enthusiasm that makes everything you do in life worthwhile.

---

## The Whole Is Greater Than The Sum Of The Parts

As a physician, I'm accustomed to examining things very closely. So let's put enthusiasm on the dissecting table and see what it's made of. It turns out that enthusiasm is such a very special feeling because it's a bundle of great qualities all rolled together to make one gigantic virtue. When you're enthusiastic you're also . . .

**Cheerful** because life is a joy.
**Confident** that things will go your way. If not today, tomorrow.
**Trusting** of others.
**Determined** to overcome obstacles.
**Bold** enough to tackle the impossible.
**Proud** of yourself and your accomplishments.
**Giving** of yourself, your time, talents and love to others.
Full of **Love** for life.

Good cheer, confidence, trust, determination, boldness, justifiable pride, willingness to give and love: These are some of the parts of enthusiasm. Each by itself is a virtue. Together they form enthusiasm, and the whole they make is greater than the sum of their goodly parts.

## Be Prepared With Enthusiasm

Writing the section above reminded me of my Scout days and my old Scout leader, a very enthusiastic man. (He wasn't that old, although he seemed ancient to us 13-year-olds.) I had to stop writing and rummage through my box of mementos to see if I could find my Boy Scout ID card. I found it, faded and wrinkled, at the bottom of the box: Arnold Fox, Troop 253, South Philadelphia. Patrol leader, 1942.

You know what I remember most about Mr. Fonoroff, our leader? His enthusiasm. He was everything a Scout is supposed to be: trustworthy, loyal, helpful, friendly, courteous, kind and cheerful. Put that all together and what do you have? Enthusiasm!

Mr. Fonoroff's favorite Scout virtue was cheerfulness. I don't know how many times we stood, all lined up, to recite section number eight of the Scout Law: "A Scout is cheerful. He smiles whenever he can. His obedience to orders is prompt and cheery. He never shirks nor grumbles at hardships."

We kids didn't know it, and perhaps Mr. Fonoroff didn't know it either, but that little saying we repeated over and over is an affirmation. We were affirming to ourselves that we were cheerful. Everytime we said "A Scout is cheerful", our subconscious mind added: "I'm a Scout, therefore, I'm cheerful. And if a Scout smiles whenever he can, I'll smile whenever *I* can. Since Scouts never shirk or grumble at hardships, I'll cheerfully tackle every job that comes my way."

With this little saying, this affirmation, we were telling ourselves how to think, act, walk, talk, believe and behave. We were writing this good information into our subconscious mind, making it a part of ourselves. How could we help but be enthusiastic?

I don't remember how to tie a square knot, read contour maps or distinguish between bracken ferns and common ferns. But I've always remembered that I'm cheerful. I can't help it: I affirmed my cheerfulness too many times to ever forget. (I also stepped in poison ivy too many times to forget what that's like too.)

---

Be prepared for life with never-ending supplies of enthusiasm.

---

## To Be Enthusiastic . . .

The secret to enthusiasm can be summed up in two words: Act enthusiastic. With all your heart and with all your soul, act enthusiastic!

*Tell* yourself what to think: enthusiastic thoughts. *See* yourself, in your mind's eye, living life with a *joie de vivre*, a high-spirited joy of life. *Think* of yourself as being an enthusiastic person. Imagine yourself walking with a bounce in your step. Think about how great you'll look and feel with a big smile on your face. Picture yourself loving life. *Feel* the enthusiasm energizing your body, mind and spirit.

Tell, see, think and feel: That'll get things started. Now put it into action. Walk with that bounce in your step. If you don't feel it there, put it there. Keep a smile on your face. If it doesn't come naturally yet, slap it on and keep it on. Speak and move with enthusiastic energy all day long. In other words, change your behavior in the desired direction. Your body will respond by revving up the "E-spot", and soon your actions will be your reality.

---

Walk, talk, act and behave enthusiastically. In no time at all you'll **be** enthusiastic!

---

## Talking Enthusiasm

To help you walk, talk, act and behave with great enthusiasm, I want you to recite the affirmation for enthusiasm I'm going to give you.

An affirmation is a verbal statement describing how you feel about yourself, others and life, and how you see the world. The little section of the Scout's Law I repeated so many times as a kid was an affirmation, a way of telling my subconscious exactly how I was supposed to think and act.

An affirmation is a way of seeing yourself as you desire yourself to be.

An affirmation is an instruction to your subconscious that must be acted upon.

When using affirmations, affirm that what you want to happen has already happened: You're already enthusiastic. Affirm only the positive, and keep your affirmation in mind at all times. Write it down on an index card or piece of paper so you can look at it often. If you're embarrassed that others might see it, write it in a code that only you understand.

Here's your affirmation for enthusiasm:

---

*I'm loaded with enthusiasm! I smile a big smile all day long because I'm glad to be living my life. I feel great because things are going my way. I'm full of love for life and love for others. Most of all, I'm always cheerful, because my life is a never-ending source of joy.*

---

I tell my patients to repeat their affirmation for enthusiasm — all their affirmations, in fact — all day long. In the morning, on the way to work, during work breaks and lunch, on the way home, in the evening and before you go to bed, repeat your affirmations over and over. Say them out loud and say them to yourself. You can't say them enough.

## Say And See

When you say your affirmation for enthusiasm, I want you to see yourself with your mind's eye acting enthusiastically. See that big smile on your face. See yourself cheerful and smiling when you wake up, when you're on your way to work, when you're at work, or with your friends and family, when you relax, when you do every and any thing. Picture yourself with that big smile. When you say that you're full of love for others, see yourself with your loved ones, sharing love. And when you say life is a never-ending source of joy, mentally review all the joyful moments in your life.

---

Say it with affirmations, and see it with visualizations. Say and see yourself as having unlimited enthusiasm, love and joy.

---

## Now *Give* Enthusiasm

A fortyish woman, a very active executive, once came to see me complaining that she had felt run-down for the past four months. "I've been from doctor to doctor," she said, "without satisfaction."

After performing a thorough physical examination, a complete personal and medical history, the appropriate laboratory studies and a review of her answers to the Purpose In Life and other tests, I explained to this woman there was no organic explanation for her feeling run-down. The problem was most likely a lack of spirit, an absence of enthusiasm in her life: anenthusiasma.

"What about my fatigue?" she asked.

"That's also due to the anenthusiasma."

"You're right," she sighed. "I haven't any enthusiasm. I wish I had some of yours."

"I'm going to give you some of mine," I said, touching my fingers to my chest. Then I turned my hand outward, fingers toward her, and thrust my hand forward, stopping it a few inches from the woman. "There! There's some enthusiasm for you!"

She laughed. "I can almost feel it."

Several months later the same woman returned to my office and said, "I want some of the same treatment you gave me last time. It made me feel great."

I looked at her chart: No treatment was marked down, other than a discussion of stress and nutrition, plus recommendations for changing her outlook on life.

"Refresh my memory," I said, somewhat embarrassed. "What treatment did I give you?"

"That gesture!" she exclaimed. "You gave me enthusiasm with that gesture!"

Isn't it marvelous how the human mind converts positive thoughts to good health?

---

Give some enthusiasm to everyone you meet. Don't worry about running out — you can't. Every time you give enthusiasm, you get just as much back, if not more.

---

## Double Your Enthusiasm By Giving Some Away

Everytime I give my patients a pep talk on enthusiasm, I feel great! Not only because I'm helping someone, but because in giving enthusiasm, I get enthusiasm. I feel the tingle up and down my spine that tells me my "E-spot" is pouring out the endorphins.

They say that a joy shared is a joy doubled. To this we can add: Enthusiasm given is enthusiasm received. Why? Because when you demonstrate to others how to be enthusiastic, you're acting enthusiastically. You're stimulating your own "E-spot". Remember, your "E-spot" responds solely to the presence of thoughts. Buried deep within your brain, lacking eyes and ears of its own, the "E-spot" has no idea what's happening outside the body. It doesn't know whether you're at the movies, driving in your car, asleep in bed, receiving the Nobel Prize or wrestling a polar bear. All it knows is that certain thoughts are in your head. When it sees any thought labeled "enthusiasm", "cheerfulness", "joy", "love", or any other positive thought, the "E-spot" grabs hold of that good notion and converts it into endorphins and other substances of health and happiness. The "E-spot" doesn't ask how the thought got there or whether it belongs: It simply responds to the good news.

So give enthusiasm to someone else and to yourself. Think enthusiasm. Walk, talk, act and behave enthusiastically. You can't go wrong with enthusiasm.

Enthusiasm, the first of the five cardinal virtues, is the "mother's milk" of health, happiness and success in life. Fill your cup to the brim with enthusiasm, for in so doing, you're filling your life to the brim with health and joy.

# Believe Yourself To Health

*. . . all things are possible to him that believeth.*

*Mark 9:23*

As a doctor, it has been my sad duty to inform many a patient that he or she is suffering from a terrible disease. Back in the early 1960s, I had to tell a 54-year-old mother of three that she had cancer, and that the outlook was grim. But instead of responding with tears or anger or disbelief, as most patients did, this woman simply smiled and said:

"If you have faith, even as small as a tiny mustard seed, nothing is impossible."

"What do you mean?" I asked, puzzled.

"That's a quote from the Scriptures," she explained. "It tells me that as long as I have belief, I can shake off cancer."

Frankly, I thought she was a little nutty. Did she really think belief could beat cancer? I knew for a fact that her cancer was growing larger and more deadly every day. I also knew, for a fact, that her cancer was inoperable.

Finally I knew, for a fact, that people in her condition had only an average of six months to live. Belief would not — could not — cure cancer. But if it made her happy to think about belief, well, I felt that was her privilege.

The next day I came into her hospital room to discuss her treatment with her. She was sitting up in bed, praying.

"Were you asking God to get rid of the cancer?" I asked impulsively when she had finished.

"No," she smiled. "I'm thanking Him for giving me such a healthy body."

"A healthy body?!" I thought. "You're dying of cancer."

Perhaps she sensed my thoughts, for she said: "In the Scriptures it says: 'According to your beliefs so shall you be treated.' I believe I'm healthy."

"What about the cancer?" I asked, still skeptical.

"It exists; it's in me. But I refuse to believe it will hurt me. I believe I'm healthy. And I know the cancer will go away," she replied gently, with a smile.

Much to my surprise, her cancer *did* go away, and she lived another ten years in good health. I certainly didn't cure the cancer. Was it the treatment she received? Even the doctors administering the therapy doubted it would do any good. What made the cancer shrink and vanish?

## The Doctor Called Spirit

*The spirit of a man will sustain his infirmity,*
*but a wounded spirit who can bear?*

*Proverbs 18:14*

This woman with her faith was one of many patients who have taught me that there is a whole realm of medicine we physicians know nothing of. We doctors can quote chapter and verse on anatomy, biochemistry, physiology, pharmacology and other scientific subjects, but we are sadly unfamiliar with the miraculous healing powers of the human mind.

Each of us is born with something special inside of us — call it God, call it karma, call it what you will. I like to refer to that special something as the spirit.

Your spirit is your spark of life, that controlling force within you that directs your life, physically, mentally and emotionally.

Your spirit is the inner you. We can neither touch nor describe the spirit, but we know it determines how you see the world.

Your spirit is that intangible something that tells every cell in your body how to behave, whether to be active and vibrant, or lethargic and distressed.

Your spirit is your power, your will to determine whether you will be healthy or sick, enthusiastic or depressed, a success or a failure.

From birth to death, your spirit directs your life. What controls your spirit? You do, through your thoughts and actions.

---

You have within you a doctor called spirit, a powerful physician capable of telling even the smallest of body cells how to behave. Your spirit is under your direct control. You tell your spirit how to behave.

---

## Belief Is The Eye of Your Spirit

*If your eye is pure, there will be sunshine in your soul. But if your eye is clouded with evil thoughts and desires, you are in deep spiritual darkness.*

*(Matthew 6:22-23)*

Your belief is the "eye" of your spirit. What you see (believe in) is what you get. If you see health, happiness and success, your spirit will respond to that great vision by setting in motion biochemical events that lead to increased energy, productivity and health.

It doesn't matter how much money you have, how old you are, what your sex is, what color you are or how much you weigh. Education and background are not important. What counts is your belief in yourself: That's the key to success. The woman with cancer believed in herself and in her good health. She saw only health and happiness for herself. Not a jot of negativity was allowed to pollute her mind. Acting on her great belief, her spirit prompted the necessary changes in body chemistry, spurred on the immune system and crushed the cancer.

What is belief in yourself? Is it an egotistical, self-centered conceit? No. It is a quiet but firm acknowledgment of your importance. Importance to what? To the nation, the economy, the firm, the family? None of these. You are important without respect to anyone or anything else. You are important because you are alive. Whether other people think differently is irrelevant; yours is the only opinion that counts. Rich or poor; black, white, brown or yellow; educated or ignorant; powerful or powerless; you are important. And you deserve the best of health and happiness.

---

Your spirit relies on your vision of the world to direct it into action. Tell your spirit the world is good, and your spirit will respond by promoting health and joy.

---

## If You Knew You Couldn't Fail . . .

Can belief in yourself take you out of the losing rut you've been in for so long? Can belief in yourself help you break out of the pattern of unhappy relationships?

Can belief help you get out of the succession of jobs you don't like, jobs you're doing just for the money, or because you feel you can't do anything else anyway? Can belief in yourself help turn your health around? Can belief help you live life joyfully and to its fullest? Can belief change a loser into a winner?

You bet it can!

I'm writing this on a very special day, one that I will remember and treasure forever. This is the day Eric, my second son, got married. It's late at night. The ceremony and reception are over, the tin cans have been tied to the back of the car, and Eric and his bride have driven off to begin their honeymoon.

This morning — it seems so long ago — Eric and I were reliving the time eight years ago when he was preparing to take an important examination. He had to pass this test in order to get into medical school.

Eric had hemmed and hawed about signing up for the test, finally admitting that he didn't have confidence in himself. "There's no way I can pass that test," he had said. "I'm not smart enough. What am I going to do when I walk in there?"

I had told him to think about how he would feel if he *knew* he was going to pass the test — that there was no way he could fail. How would he feel if he *knew* that he would not only pass, but would get the highest possible score? "How would you feel if you knew you were a success?" I had asked him.

"I'd feel great," came Eric's reply.

"Well," I told him, "I want you to study hard, and to walk, talk, think, believe and act as if you've already passed the test. I want you to walk, talk, think, believe and act as if you've already been accepted into medical school."

Needless to say, Eric did pass the exam. Here he was, eight years later, a medical doctor about to be married. "I've never forgotten what you told me, Dad," he said. "There have been times when I doubted myself, and let that hold me back. Then I remember what you told me and it's as if my belief in myself makes me ten times as smart and ten times as strong as I am."

Does belief in yourself really make you smarter? Let me put it this way: You're smarter, stronger and more talented than you think you are. But doubt, fear and hesitation have tightly bound your talents in chains. The key to freedom, then, is belief in yourself. Something wonderful happens when you believe in yourself. Your eyes are better able to find solutions and to see beauty, quicker to spot opportunity. All the circuits in your brain open wide, allowing the knowledge and wisdom already there to circulate freely. Emotional channels open wide, allowing you to love and be loved, to enjoy life to the fullest. All your talents are mustered by belief; they're brought together into a great army called success, success in every aspect of your life.

When I was in medical school, 30 years ago, we were taught that it was possible to change your life, if, and only if, you carefully examined your belief system through years of analysis and therapy. Only then would your life change. As soon as I got out of medical school, I discarded that impractical and unnecessary approach. You don't have to dig into every crevice of your brain trying to discover what your mother or father did or did not say to you 37 years ago. Just believe in yourself. Believe in your great ability to succeed. Believe that you deserve the best life has to offer. Now couple your belief with action, and you're on your way.

---

If you knew you couldn't fall, your spirit would always be looking for success — and would find it!

---

## The 51% Solution

One patient, a 63-year-old woman suffering from heart disease, looked at me incredulousy when I encouraged her to always believe in herself.

"Dr. Fox," she said, "your theory is fine but reality is sometimes pretty harsh. Only a Pollyanna could believe in herself 100%, 100% of the time."

How can anybody believe 100% in themselves, 100% of the time? That's difficult to do. Luckily, you don't have to. If you can believe in yourself even 51%, 51% of the time, you've made a good start. Fifty-one percent is enough to change your behavior, enough to get you acting, thinking, walking and talking as if you already were a success. Your new behavior will be reflected in improved health of mind and body, encouraging you to believe even more. Remember, what you see is what you get. Start believing in yourself today.

Here's a young woman who put the 51% solution to good use. We met about seven years ago when I filled in for a vacationing doctor at his office, miles away from mine. One of the patients I saw was a 25-year-old woman who had had surgery for cancer of the breast a few years before. The cancer had returned, but she was refusing to have another surgery or undergo other treatment. I encouraged her to get medical care, but she wanted to know if there was anything else I could suggest.

"I heard you talking about the power of the mind with that man in the waiting room. Is there anything about my mind I can use to beat my cancer?"

I said yes, but I couldn't recommend it as the sole treatment for cancer. She quickly assured me that she would go back to the cancer specialist if I would tell her about the power of the mind.

After explaining the relationship between the mind and the immune system, I asked her to picture the disease-fighting cells in her body — T-cells and phagocytes (fag-o-sites) — as powerful little fish with big teeth.

"There are millions and millions of these little fish swimming all around your body," I said. "Their job is to destroy cancer and other diseases. Now imagine that your cancer is a big grey mass, or better yet, a big piece of grey blubber. Picture all those little fish with their big, sharp teeth — millions and millions of them — swarming over the grey blubber, biting out chunks, ripping it to pieces. See them and know that you have mobilized your immune system. See them as the army, navy, marines and air force swooping down on the enemy, blasting him to bits. Wave after wave they attack, pulling off pieces of the grey blubber and taking them to the liver, where the cancer is ground up and destroyed forever. Bit by bit, picture the cancer shrinking until it finally vanishes. But it can come back again, so you must imagine the fish destroying the grey blubber every day, once in the morning, once in the evening.

"With this technique," I told her, "you are telling your body that it has the power to destroy the cancer. If you believe that — really believe it — your body will respond with renewed strength and vigor to fight the disease. In addition to visualizing your 'little fish with big teeth' eating up the cancer, you should walk, talk, think and act as if your body had already taken care of the problem. Success begins with belief. Your thoughts and actions help determine your beliefs, so think and act as if what you want is already yours."

She was excited. "Dr. Fox," she said with a smile, "I like that approach. I believe it can work."

Then her smile quickly faded, "But if it doesn't, I'm in trouble."

"That's why you should go back to the cancer specialist. Use the power of the mind as an adjunct."

Out of the blue, seven years later, the same woman showed up in my office, a big smile on her face. "I don't want you to treat me because I'm not sick. I want you to look and tell me if you can find any trace of that cancer I had last time."

I examined her carefully and performed the appropriate tests. There was no sign of cancer.

"I started out to do what you told me to do. I imagined the fish eating the cancer twice a day, and I started with the cancer doctors. But the treatment made me so sick, I couldn't go on. I decided to go with what you told me, even though I was kind of scared. Keeping up my belief was hard. It was hard to believe that my body could beat the cancer, like you said it could. But I imagined the fish everyday, and soon I started to feel better. The lump in my breast went away. I didn't go back to see you because I thought you'd disapprove of my not going to the other doctors. But I want you to see for yourself that the cancer's gone."

Now, I'm not saying that imagining the "fish" eating her cancer cured her. Perhaps the cancer treatment she'd begun, even if she didn't see it through, was responsible. Or maybe there was spontaneous remission, with the body taking care of the cancer all by itself. But my 30 years of experience in the front lines of crisis medicine, treating the sickest of patients in the intensive care units and coronary care units, have convinced me that the human mind is a powerful weapon against disease. We haven't completely mastered its use, and we can't always tell which person will benefit most from its power. But we do know it paves the way for success.

---

If you can believe in yourself, even 51% of the time, your spirit will begin turning disease to health, depression to happiness and failure to success.

---

## Belief Is Contagious

*If I am not for myself, who will be? But if I am only for myself, what am I? And if not now, when?*

*Hillel*

Frank Lloyd Wright, the great architect and one of the most original thinkers in America, once said: "The things always happen that you believe in. And belief is the thing that makes them happen. And I think nothing will happen until you thoroughly and deeply believe in it."

For years I traveled the speakers' circuit, talking to doctors, salespeople, managerial groups and corporate executives in the big and small cities of the United States, Canada and Australia. Generally I would discuss stress, nutrition, the immune system and the effect of the mind on the body in the first part of my talk, saving motivation, inspiration, belief and enthusiasm for the end.

I loved the banquets that were held in the evenings. Not for the food but because I often got to hear Bob Richards, one of the great speakers of all times. You may remember Bob Richards as the gold-medal Olympic athlete. I usually sat with him at the head table, listening carefully to his talks. I heard him speak many times but I never got tired of listening for his message rang so true. And the message was that belief is a vital part of every accomplishment.

One story he told went something like this. It was the 1950s, and the world's record for the mile run was a little over four minutes. Four minutes: that was the magic barrier no one had been able to crack. Many had tried but none succeeded. And none would succeed, said the experts, for the human body is simply incapable of running the mile in less than four minutes. Given the way our arms, legs, muscles, lungs, hearts were, it simply could not be done. People, including runners, believed that the four-minute mile was impossible. It was a dream, a fantasy.

A young English medical student named Roger Bannister, however, believed he could do it. He trained, ran, acted and behaved as if it were possible to break the four-minute mile. Of course, you know what happened. He went out to the track one day and proved that man could run a mile in less than four minutes. The critics and scoffers said it was a fluke, an accident, no one would ever do it again. But now the other young runners knew it could be done! Now they believed that *they* could do it. With feet made fleet by belief, they proved the four-minute barrier was no barrier at all. Within a few months the four-minute mile barrier was broken twice again. Today you're considered slow if it takes you a whole four mintues to run a mile. Today's top runners have set their sights on a three-minute, 30 second mile.

What had happened? Did runners suddenly evolve faster bodies or longer legs or stronger sets of lungs? Absolutely not! The only thing that changed was their belief. When they believed they couldn't do it, they couldn't do it. Roger Bannister believed he could break the magic barrier. He did it. Others believed that they could do it, too. And they did.

---

If you believe you can't do something, you'll never do it.
Believe you can, however, and you've all but done it.

---

## Thank God (But Don't Bother Him)

*Lift up thine eyes and look from the place*
*where you are.*

*Genesis 13:14, 15*

People often ask me how God and prayer fit into my scheme of belief. I tell them that prayer is wonderful, but that they shouldn't bother God!

In the Scriptures we read: "Whatsoever things you desire, when you pray, believe you receive them and you shall have them" (Matthew 11:24). Some of my patients have asked me what this passage means. Will belief alone make you successful in life? No. Belief sets up the conditions that make success, health and happiness possible. To turn potential into reality, you must *do* something about it.

Just last week a 35-year-old woman who had immigrated from Poland several years before came to my office. She felt weak, tired and depressed, and had been suffering from a series of colds and flus. Lab studies showed that her immune system was weak, but not dangerously so.

"Back in Poland," she said to me, "things were better. Here I am poor; I have nothing. And Dr. Fox, I've given up. I don't think anything good is going to happen to me. Back home, I prayed to God everyday for freedom. He gave me freedom. Now I pray to God to give me money. He hasn't given me any. Sometimes I think that God is back in Poland, otherwise he would answer my prayers."

I asked if she did anything else besides pray to God to give her money. "Have you asked for a raise? Looked for a new job? Considered retraining? Tried to open your own business? Sought out new opportunities?" She replied that she'd done none of these things: She'd simply prayed for money. "I'm too poor, too tired. What could I possibly do?"

"The first thing," I told her, "is to stop looking at yourself as being so poor and helpless. A loser looks at himself and sees all the problems. But a winner sees the tremendous potential.

"Lift up thine eyes to the stars. If the stars are too far for you to reach right now, fine. Lift up thine eyes and look around for a ladder.

"You're poor? Well, you're in good company, because most of the people in this country came from low financial backgrounds. Growing up, many of us had little money — but we weren't poor. 'Poor' is poverty of the spirit. You can have empty pockets but not be poor if you are rich in spirit, if you believe in yourself.

"How does a poor person become money-rich? By looking to the future. By following great dreams, by chasing rainbows, by believing they can reach the stars.

If you're rich in spirit, you can never be poor. If you're rich in determination, nothing can hold you back. If you're rich in enthusiasm, success is near. And it all begins with belief. Believe you have the power, the ability, the intelligence, the imagination, the perseverance, the strength, the cleverness, the whatever it takes to succeed — and you're on your way to success. You believed before when you came to this country all by yourself. Believe again."

"Should I stop praying?" she asked.

"No," I answered. "Keep praying. But stop bothering God. Give thanks to God for giving you a brain, a strong back and all the ability you need to succeed. Thank Him for giving you the tools. Then get out there and take the necessary steps to get yourself more money."

I looked at her, wondering if she would tell me I was crazy. But she smiled and I could see the determination in her eye as she said: "You know what, Dr. Fox? I can do it. I'm going to do it. I'm going to thank God for giving me the tools and stop begging for a handout. I know it's going to work."

Needless to say, she found the strength and courage to demand a substantial raise from her boss. When he refused, she quit on the spot, a daring thing to do considering her lack of financial resources.

"It was probably a stupid thing to do," she later told me, "but it made me feel like I was in control of my life. I got the first job I applied for, with a much better salary. I think I got it because the boss could see what a determined person I was."

Her physical and emotional problems disappeared almost immediately. A recheck of her immune system showed that it was in tip-top shape.

"No more colds for me," she said, laughing. "I'm too busy making money to be sick."

---

Believers always know where to look — forward.

---

## Believers Don't Look For Free Rides . . .

. . . because they don't need them. Besides, they know that there's no such thing as a free ride. There's always a price to pay, somewhere, sometime. The dispirited woman from Poland was looking for a free ride. She wanted something for nothing. But the woman with cancer, the one I described at the beginning of this chapter, wasn't asking God or anyone else for a favor. She simply thanked God for her good health. In thanking God for her health, she affirmed that she already had good health. In other words, she acted, prayed *and believed* that she already had what she wanted. And she got it.

---

God helps those who help themself. Pray, give thanks, then get to work!

---

## Apple Power

Several years ago I put the power of belief to work with Little League baseball players. Somehow I wound up serving as assistant coach for one of the teams at the local park. The coach was an intelligent and skillful young man who had the boys running through all kinds of drills during spring training. They were batting, throwing, running, pitching and playing like little champs as the season approached.

Opening day finally came and the high-spirited, enthusiastic boys — some of whom were barely bigger than the bats they swung — charged out onto the field. I never saw a more excited group of kids. These kids believed they were winners. You could hear it in their conversations and in their confident predictions of victory, in their walk. You could see it in their eyes. They were bragging about how many home runs they would hit, and making bets as to who would make the most spectacular play in the field. They looked, acted and felt like winners.

The other team didn't know what hit them that first game. We easily won the next several games and were considered *the* team to beat in the league. Then something unexpected happened: We lost. The worst team in the league beat us. Then we stunned everyone by losing the next game, and the next: Soon we had lost six in a row. The effect on the boys was devastating. Our batters couldn't seem to hit the ball anymore, the fielders made error after error and the pitchers were wild.

You should have seen the change in the boys' attitudes. The enthusiasm and backslapping were gone. They straggled to the park late for practice, and slunk out of the park as soon as the game was over. They stopped wearing their team uniforms to school because they didn't want anyone to know they were on a losing team.

"No sense trying," one boy told me. "We always lose. We're always going to lose." The team became more and more inept. Their morale hit rock bottom as we became the laughing stock of the league.

I helped the listless boys run through the warmup exercises before the next game, then watched as one of the mothers gave the boys a pre-game snack consisting of sugary doughnuts and Coke. It suddenly hit me. I had an answer to their problem. It had to do with belief, and, in this case, the junk food. All that sugar they ate before the game was giving them a quick rush of energy, then a big drop as their body reacted to the excess sugar by driving down their blood sugar — and their energy levels. I asked the coach to let me take charge for the game. He agreed. I sent my son Barry, who was in the stands, to the market for a big bag of apples. Then I walked into the dugout and said:

"Hold it, boys. Don't eat that junk!"

They looked at me as if I were crazy. Not only were they the worst team in the league, now they were to be punished, they thought, by having their snack taken away.

"There are two reasons why we are losing," I told them. "One is mental. We think we're losers, so we lose. The other is physical. This junk food you've been eating saps your energy."

They looked at me like I was some kind of nut. "Let's throw out all the junk food," I said as I grabbed a trash can and walked along the dugout, urging them to throw out their doughnuts, sodas and candy bars.

"We're not losing because we're no good. You're the best team in the league — you proved that in the beginning of the season. We beat all the good teams easily. We're going to turn things around right now. Let's all sit on the bench and close our eyes. I want everyone to imagine themselves standing at the plate, ready to bat. Picture yourself at the plate. Now think to yourself 'I'm going to hit that ball! I'm going to hit it so far, the other team's not going to catch it.' See yourself stand at the plate, batting. See how tough you look standing there. Imagine the pitcher. He's worried. He knows you're going to hit the ball. Imagine the fielders — they're backing up because they know you're a great hitter. OK. Keep your eyes closed. Imagine the pitcher winding up, throwing the ball. You can see the ball as it leaves his hand. You can see it clearly. It comes over the plate and you swing the bat. See your bat hitting the ball. Imagine the ball flying through the air! Can you see that?"

I have to admit that the reaction was mixed. Some boys responded enthusiastically, some did not. But I felt it was a good start. The umpire called for the game to begin.

I looked from one to the other. "You're all good baseball players. But you have to believe in yourselves. You've got to walk, talk and act like great ball players. See yourself, in your mind, as the great player you are."

"Coach, is it OK if I see myself hitting a home run?" asked Sam, the biggest player on the team.

"It's OK for you, but the rest of you just think about hitting the ball and getting on safely."

"Coach," Sam said, hopping excitedly from one foot to the other, "I'm gonna do it! I saw myself hitting a home run, and I'm going to hit one! Watch!"

"Remember. If you believe you can do it, then you can do it!" I said.

"But coach!" protested Ronnie, our star pitcher, "why couldn't we have our soda?" And as he hurried out to the pitcher's mound I heard him mumble: "Some coach!"

I don't know why I hadn't realized sooner that their lack of belief was hampering their play on the field. Like many of the patients I've seen over the years, the boys had predisposed themselves to failure. In later games I would explain to them that you are what you think you are. Believe you are a failure, and you will surely fail. But believe you are a winner, and success is within your grasp.

The game began. Our opponents were not really that good, but we made some fielding errors and quickly found ourselves two runs behind. I noticed, however, that Sam and a couple of the other boys were playing with the same enthusiasm they had had at the beginning of the season. Ronnie struck out the last two batters and it was our turn to hit.

The boys returned to the dugout to select their bats and helmets as Barry came running up with a big bag of apples. "See this?" I asked, holding up an apple. "This is what you should be eating. Not doughnuts, apples! Apples are full of the nutrition winners need to keep their body strong. This apple has vitamins and minerals to help you win games. From now on we're going to eat apples before every game. We're the Apple Power team.

With belief and nutrition on our side, we can't lose! I
want everyone to say it: Are we winners?"

A few of them shouted, "Yes."

"Winners have more enthusiasm!" I said. "Are we
winners?"

"Yes!" they shouted. Well, most of them shouted.

"Everybody has to believe it for it to work. Let's hear
it for Apple Power!"

"Apple Power!"

"From now on that's our slogan: Apple Power. Apple
Power stands for belief in ourselves and good nutrition.
We're going to win because we believe in Apple Power!"
I shouted.

"Nice speech, Doc," the umpire said, hand on his hips.
"Do you mind if we play baseball?"

Little Steve stepped up to the plate. "Apple Power!" I
shouted. "Apple Power!" echoed Sam. Steve looked
embarrassed as some of the boys on the other team
snickered. The pitcher threw the ball. Steve hit a
grounder up the middle for a single. Alan, one of our
best hitters, stepped up to the plate.

"Apple Power!" I shouted. This time several of the
boys yelled with me. Alan ignored us. He slapped the
first pitch to left field, advancing Steve to third base.
Now Sam, our biggest and strongest player, stepped up
to bat. He had been knocking the ball back to the fence
early in the season, although for the last six games had
not been hitting very well. But I could see a difference in
his stance, in his attitude. There was confidence in his
stride, in his eye — a confidence I hadn't seen for a long
time. The pitcher wound up, threw a sizzling fast ball.
Sam belted it over the fence for a three-run home run.

And that was all it took to turn a bunch of dispirited
losers into enthusiastic winners. The primary difference
was their belief. They were no better, no more skillful
with bat and ball than they had been minutes ago. No,
the difference was belief. Their self-confidence and self-
image improved dramatically as we won game after
game. (Also, the boys' mothers were forbidden to hand

out junk food at the park. Instead, we ate apples and drank fruit juice before each game.)

We spent five minutes before every game seeing ourselves, in our minds' eyes, as winners. We imagined ourselves hitting the ball hard, making great plays in the field and pitching strikeouts. In other words, we practiced believing in ourselves. I spoke to the boys about goals, and the importance of always keeping our goals in front of us so we know where we're headed. All the boys were given a card on which I had written: "I know that I am a good baseball player, and I know that I'm a winner!" They were instructed to carry their card with them, and look at it often during the day. I gave Ronnie, our star pitcher, an extra card which said: "Pitch low and hard."

With the boys' parents behind me, encouraging their sons to believe in themselves, we won game after game. Unfortunately, because of the six consecutive losses, we could not recapture first place. Our last game of the season was against the Reds, the first place team. They had trounced us in an earlier game. This time we played superbly. Our batters knocked out seven runs in five innings, and Ronnie was working on a no-hitter. Before each pitch, he pulled a little card out of his back pocket and looked at it. This went on for five innings. I didn't say anything, but I was curious. What was on the card, and why was he looking at it before each pitch? Finally, I had to know. In the middle of the fifth inning, after Ronnie had struck out the first two batters, I called time out and walked to the mound.

"What's on that card?" I asked. Ronnie showed me the card I had given him, the one which said: "Pitch low and hard." Forgetting what I had told him, and speaking as an assistant coach, not as a doctor, I said:

"Why do you have to look at it all the time? Can't you memorize what it says?"

Ronnie looked absolutely disgusted. He put his hands on his hips, looked up at me and shook his head: "But coach," he said, "you told me to always keep my goals in front of me!"

He was right. He always knew what he wanted to do: It was on his card. Well, we finished up the season by beating the first place team. The boys felt great, but more importantly, they learned an important lesson: If you walk, talk and act like a loser, you *are* a loser. But if you believe in yourself, success is sure to follow. After the season, when I ran into the boys' parents at the markets in Beverly Hills, they told me that the motivation and belief these Little Leaguers learned had carried over into their school and home lives. They're carrying forth the magic of self-belief.

## Tell Your Spirit What To Believe

*In any project, the most important factor is your belief. Without belief there can be no successful outcome. That is fundamental.*

*William James*

You are what you believe you are, what you feel you are, what you say you are. Believe that you're sickly, and you're welcoming disease with open arms. Feel that you're unhappy, and you've taken the joy away from your heart. Say that you're a loser, and you've already lost in life. But act, feel, believe and say that you are healthy and happy, as the woman with cancer did with such determination, and you'll set in motion the events that spur health and happiness. Belief is a self-fulfilling prophecy.

When you believe you're a failure, it's as if you erected a giant billboard right in front of your face. In big letters right across the billboard it says: "You're a failure. You're nothing." That billboard's there 24 hours a day, reminding you that you're a loser. And there's a record player in your head playing the "Failure Song" over and over all day and all night, brain-washing you. Your spirit can't help but believe that you're a failure.

Paint a new billboard in front of your eyes, one that says, "I'm a success! I believe I can do it! Every cell in my body is working overtime toward my success!" Put a new record on your mental stereo, one that sings, "I'm a success!" *That* record will open your eyes and mind to the possibilities that are yours. *These* are the messages you want to keep in front of you at all times.

Use this affirmation for belief to enthusiastically bring the positive message home to your spirit:

---

*Belief is the eye of the spirit, and my spirit sees nothing but good because I believe in myself. Body, mind and spirit, I believe that I deserve the best life has to offer. With every word, thought and action, I demonstrate my great belief in myself.*

---

## Let Faith Transform You

It's said that "Faith can transform a slender willow into an iron pillar." When you believe in yourself, enthusiastically believe in yourself, your great faith gives your spirit the strength of iron — and much more.

Keep your mind's eye clear and your body filled with the shining light of belief. Believe that you are a worthwhile person. Believe that you deserve great health, bountiful happiness and much success. Believe that with all your heart.

Now take it a step further: Believe that you are *already* in excellent health, full of happiness and successful in life. If you don't yet have the belief, pretend you do. Act as if you do, walk as if you do, talk as if you believe in yourself. Fool your spirit into thinking you're a believer.

The woman with cancer believed. She told her spirit exactly how to act. She insisted that her spirit see things her way, and she beat that cancer. Her brave example shows the way. That way begins with belief.

CHAPTER

# The Healing Chemistry Of Love

*Love is a fruit in all seasons, and within the reach of every hand.*

*Mother Teresa*

Let me tell you about a patient named Joannie, a 25-year-old woman referred to me by a fellow doctor who explained, "I don't know what's wrong with her, Arnie. I think she's a chronic complainer."

Later she told me with a wry smile, "I was born to save my parent's marriage but it didn't work."

"What happened?"

"Nothing. They stayed together for my sake, kept a stiff upper lip and raised me."

"Did they resent you for forcing them to stay together?"

"No, I don't think so. They were both very good about being parents, but they didn't love me. I was their obligation. The day I graduated from high school they split up."

I conducted a thorough physical examination, took her personal and family medical history, and performed the indicated tests. Although I found no specific disease process to account for her long history of colds and flus, her menstrual problems and her prolonged bout with mononucleosis, I did discover that her immune system was weak.

Her total white blood cell count was 4,000, which is low. Not dangerously low, but enough so that her body had a difficult time mounting a defense against invading germs. Her T4/T8 ratio was similarly depressed at 0.9 (less than one T4 "helper" cell for every T8 "suppressor" cell).

The T4/T8 ratio describes the balance between the helper cells that tell the fighting immune cells to go get the bacteria, viruses, fungi and other germs, and the suppressor cells that tell the immune system to stop fighting and cool off. You need enough helper cells to spur the immune system to battle, but not so many that it keeps on fighting after the germs have been defeated, turning on your own body when there's nothing else left to fight. That's where the suppressor cells come in: They tell the immune system when to stop fighting. If your T4/T8 ratio is high (too many helper cells compared to suppressor cells), your immune system may turn on you, leaving you with an autoimmune disease such as rheumatoid arthritis. If your T4/T8 ratio is too low (too many suppressor cells compared to helper cells), your immune system may not be able to respond adequately to germs. Low T4/T8 ratios are seen with AIDS. The good T4/T8 ratio is between 1.6 and 1.8.

Extensive tests produced no physical explanation for the lowered ratio and total T-cell count, leading me to believe that the problem lay in her thoughts.

"I knew you would say that," she replied when I explained this to her. "You're probably right."

"What's it like being raised in a loveless home?" I asked.

"A big blah," she replied sadly.

"What's life like for you now?"

"Still a big blah. It's always been a loveless blah."

"Do you love anyone now? A boyfriend?"

"I've never had a boyfriend."

"Why? You're very pretty."

All of a sudden her face melted into tears. "I can't love anyone," she sobbed. "I'm afraid."

A few minutes passed before she could compose herself.

"You've got to let some love into your life," I said.

"I'm afraid."

I touched my hand to my heart then extended it to her, symbolically giving her love with the gesture. "Here's some of my love. I'm sharing it with you." She looked at my hand kind of suspiciously. "Take it. No strings attached." Still she hesitated. "It's a gift to you because I love you."

Again she broke into sobs. "You're the first person that said they loved me."

"Your parents never said it?"

"No."

"No one has ever said they love you?"

"No."

Wow, I thought, what a horrible way to go through life! No wonder her immune system is battered.

"I'm going to play armchair psychologist and say that as a child, you interpreted your parents' lack of love for you as meaning that you were an unworthy person, a nothing. You've lacked self-esteem since before you can remember, and you felt you were unworthy of love. The light of your spirit is barely flickering. We've got to get that fire burning again, a big fire of love to warm you and everyone around you."

I held out my hands toward her as if trying to warm them before a fire. "I don't feel any heat. Say 'I love myself'."

"But I don't," she protested.

"Say it anyway," I commanded in my best "all-knowing doctor" tone of voice, "Say 'I love myself'."

"I love myself."

"Louder."

"I love myself."

"Stick out your chin. Make me believe you!"

"I love myself!" she said, a hint of a smile beginning to appear on her face.

"Right now your E-Spot is converting your enthusiasm and self-love into endorphins — even if you're faking the love. Hey, I can feel a little heat now."

She laughed. "I'm a hot woman."

"Good! Say that! Believe it! The fire of your spirit is filling this room with the warmth of your love!"

"I'm a hot woman! The fire of my spirit is filling the room with the warmth of my love!

"I feel *good*, Dr. Fox. Some of the blahness is gone."

"Great!"

Before she left my office, Joannie agreed to begin seeing, saying, feeling, acting and believing as if she were full of love. I wrote out a series of affirmations and visualizations for her, reminding her to think of herself as a "hot woman" who could fill any room with the loving fire of her spirit. The next time I saw her, six months later, her immune system was back to normal and she was feeling great.

"I've got a boyfriend," she told me, tears running from her eyes down to her big smile. "He said he loves me."

---

Love is the fire of the spirit.

---

## What Is Love?

The dictionary has a couple of definitions for love, such as *an intense affectionate concern for another person; an intense sexual desire for another person* plus (and this is the most important of the definitions), *a strong fondness or enthusiasm for something.*

When my patients confide in me that they love someone, however, they usually mean: *I love you and I want you to act and behave the way I believe you should, and if you don't, I won't love you anymore.* In other words, to many people, love means taking possession and control of another.

Real love, however, hasn't as much to do with the other person as it does with you. Love is, or should be, a projection of your good feelings onto others.

"I see goodness within me and I see it in you," you say when you truly love. "I love you for that goodness."

Love of others begins with your love for yourself. It is impossible to freely love others if you do not love yourself.

---

The love I have for others is a reflection of the love that is within me.

---

## Belief Plus Enthusiasm Equals Self-Love

What does it mean to love yourself? This is not a narcissistic self-love. I don't want you standing in front of the mirror all day asking who is the fairest in the land, or constantly bragging about how wonderful you are. No, the kind of self-love I'm referring to is an extension of belief in yourself.

You cannot love yourself unless you believe in yourself. You must believe you are a good person, worthy of the best life has to offer. You must believe in you, the person; not the income, not the family background, not the possessions, not the job. You must believe in yourself.

There's a great scene in a musical comedy called *How To Succeed In Business Without Really Trying* that shows the power of self-love. J. Pierrepoint Finch, a young man trying desperately to climb up from the mailroom to the top of the corporate ladder, sings "I Believe In You" to the washroom mirror. The scene is presented tongue-in-cheek but the message is clear: Monty believes in himself. And he succeeds.

Begin with belief, then add enthusiasm. Believe in yourself enthusiastically! Don't offer lip-service to the concept; really believe in you. Walk, talk, act and behave as if you believe in yourself enthusiastically! That's how you develop the kind of self-love that will fan the flames of your spirit.

---

Self-love, the prerequisite to being able to love others, is based on enthusiastic belief in yourself.

---

## Love Is God Within

*. . . he that dwelleth in love dwelleth in God,*
*and God in him.*

*I John 4:16*

I like to take the definition of love one step further to say that since God is love, to love means to be blessed with a spark of the divine. Remember, enthusiasm *"entheos"* means "in God," and enthusiasm is part of love. Thus, God is a part of love.

"Dr. Fox, do you literally mean that? I'm not a religious person and I can't accept that," one patient stated.

When I say that God is a part of love I mean it literally, and also in the sense that love is a compilation of all the good things in the world. Whether you interpret God in the Judeo-Christian sense, or as nature, genes or what have you, I feel confident that you can look upon love as the Creator's personal calling card.

"I'm giving you an unlimited supply of love," the Creator says to us. "Use this love for yourself, and spread it around. The more love there is in the world, the better."

If you have a problem with self-love, if you feel such an attitude exceeds the boundaries of modesty, remember that what I'm really talking about is loving the higher power that is within all of us, the God within.

---

Self-love is a acknowledgment that the Creator has made you a person worthy of love.

---

## Self-Love = Self-Image

Why is self-love so important? Aren't belief and enthusiasm enough? Must you also love yourself? Absolutely. You see, "self-love" is another way of saying "self-image" and self-image is the key to behavior, personality, health and success.

I once received a letter from an elderly man living in New Jersey. He wrote, "Life has been a succession of failures for me, in family, business and personal life. I seem to have the opposite of the Midas touch — whatever I touch turns to mud. I think of myself as being two inches tall."

This man is likely suffering from a problem I see a lot of among my patients: lack of self-love, or to put it another way, a poor self-image. Poor self-image is a serious problem, for your self-image is your mental blueprint, the foundation upon which your behavior and personality are built.

---

To love yourself is to esteem yourself.

---

## Mental Blueprints

Mental blueprints are "written" instructions to your spirit. Like the blueprint for a building or bridge, your mental blueprint is full of directions; in this case, on how to build an outlook on life. If the blueprint for an office building says "five stories tall", the building will be five stories high. If the bridge blueprint indicates the bridge is to be 30 feet above the water, the bridge will be 30 feet over the water. The instructions are followed to the letter.

What's written on your mental blueprint is likewise carefully obeyed when your worldview is constructed in your head. If a person's mental blueprint says, "I'm a nothing, I'm two inches tall. Everything I do turns out wrong," the person cannot help but act, feel, behave, walk and talk as if they are a nothing. This terrible belief is invariably reflected in their lack of success. They believe they are a failure. Their subconscious, that very reliable servant, translates the feeling into action and reality. And if something were to go right in the person's life, their subconscious would immediately sabotage it because it knows that good things cannot happen. How does the subconscious know that? Well, it says so, right on the mental blueprint. And every instruction on the blueprint must be followed to the letter.

---

What's written on your mental blueprint determines your outlook on life, your health and whether or not you will grasp your dreams.

---

## Self-Image, The Possible And The Impossible

Your self-image, your self-love, determines what is possible and impossible in your life, what you can and cannot accomplish, how many rich, beautiful experiences and feelings you can or cannot enjoy, how much love you have to share with others.

We're constantly faced with tasks, opportunities, feelings, stressors, information and other input into our lives. Let's group all this input into two categories: the possible and the impossible. The things we do, experience or handle without too much difficulty fall within our *Comfort Zone*. Those things that tax us or make us uncomfortable, plus those things we cannot do, belong to the *Tension Zone*.

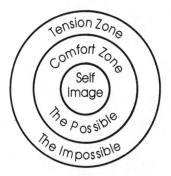

The Comfort Zone comfortably surrounds your self-image, allowing you to turn your good feelings about yourself outward into action. These are the situations, friends and feelings you're at ease with, all the ways for you to find love, happiness and success.

Wrapped tightly around the Comfort Zone, a fist squeezing hard, is the Tension Zone, those situations, people and feelings that are difficult for you to deal with — or impossible to handle. Your Tenzion Zone surrounds you with sheer walls. It's a prison locking you in and shrinking your horizons. The far end of your Tension Zone represent the absolute boundaries of your world.

How large are these two zones? That all depends on what's written in your mental blueprints. If your blueprints say, "Yes! I've got lots of self-love, I can do things, I love to experience new things," you'll have a large Comfort Zone. With a big Comfort Zone, your

Tension Zone is pushed far away. There are lots of things, people and attitudes for you to enjoy in your world.

But if your self-image is small, if your mental blueprints have "failure" scribbled all over them, your Comfort Zone will be dwarfish and your Tension Zone menacingly close. The boundaries of your world will be very close, putting a tight limit on what you can do and enjoy. Your choices will be few. Compare for yourself:

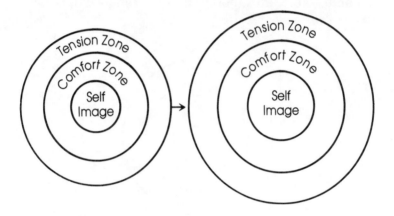

Your Tension Zone will always exist. But the larger your self-image, the greater your Comfort Zone and the more distant the tension. And the larger will your world be.

How do you increase your Comfort Zone and push the Tension Zone away? Improve your self-image. Learn to love yourself. Fill your mental blueprints with love and other good feelings.

Joannie's mental blueprint had said: "My parents don't love me. I'm not worth loving; I'm a nothing. I have no love for others." When she found herself in a situation where the question of love was raised, say, when she met an interesting young man, her subconscious read those instructions and said: "Nope! No love for Joannie." Until her blueprints were changed, she could not give love, not to herself or to others. Neither could she receive love.

A strong positive self-image makes your world comfortable
and full of the possible.

## What's Written On Your Mental Blueprints?

How large are your self-image, Comfort and Tension Zones? Are your tension boundaries far away, as they should be, or almost close enough to touch? Do you agree with these statements?

1. I am comfortable receiving compliments.
2. I like to give compliments to people who deserve them.
3. Most of the things I do turn out fairly well.
4. I usually look forward to new people or situations.
5. People enjoy having me around.
6. I get a good feeling when I see others doing well.
7. I feel that I'm in control of my life just about all the time.
8. I like myself.
9. People are generally interesting and worth knowing.

The more statements you agree with, the larger your self-image is likely to be. Your Comfort Zone is broad and your Tension Zone far away. You can handle what life throws at you because you love and trust yourself.

## Affirmation For Self-Love

Fortunately, it's possible to rewrite your mental blueprints with affirmations. Repeat this affirmation for self-esteem several times a day, until you develop the kind of self-love that makes living a pleasure.

*When I look in the mirror, I see a happy, confident, loving person who enthusiastically believes life is a banquet spread before me, waiting to be enjoyed. The fire of my spirit burns bright with love.*

Now visualize yourself being pleased. *Set aside a few quiet moments, close your eyes and see yourself with a smile on your face. With your mind's eye, see yourself happy, surrounded by people who like you. See yourself confidently handling your daily tasks. See an aura around yourself, an aura of love radiating out to touch everyone.*

Use this visualization, this visual affirmation, to strengthen your verbal affirmation.

The more you love yourself, the more you can love others.
The more you love others, the more you will be loved in return..

## Write Me As One Who Loves His Fellow Men

With plenty of self-love (that is, with a good self-image), it's easy to love others. One of my patients was a jovial 47-year-old priest. We became good friends, often caring for the same patients; me, physically, and he, spiritually. Many times we sat together in the hospital cafeteria discussing religion, philosophy and his love for the people he worked sometimes with.

"Arnold," he would say, "I wonder if I'm doing any good. I see person after person in the church, in the schools, in the settlement houses, in the hospitals. So many are lacking even the bare necessities of life. I try to arrange for them to get food, clothes, bedding, a roof over their heads, but sometimes I can't. There's so much suffering, just in our little area. I feel like King Canute, trying to push back the ocean with my hands. I wish I could solve all their problems but sometimes all they get from me is a little love and understanding. That doesn't fill their belly very well."

"Well, you love the people and you love God. Your work expresses that love."

"But am I making any difference?" he would ask. "Am I pushing back the ocean?"

"I think so. One drop of water at a time, you're creating your own ocean of love right here in the hospital, at the church, the families you help. I think you should turn some of that love you give everyone else so freely onto yourself. Appreciate your good works. The effect of your work may not be apparent to you, but it certainly is to every individual you've helped."

"I agree, but on the other hand, I'm weary with doubt," he would say. "On the other hand, I love the people I'm trying to help. They're good people who need a little help."

One day Bob invited me to a celebration the church was throwing in honor of his twenty-fifth year as a priest. Of course, my wife Hannah and I attended. To my great surprise, I was Bob's guest of honor. "Shouldn't you have one of your priest friends or a church official as your guest of honor?" I asked as Bob seated me beside him at the head table.

"You're my best friend, Arnold, for you've always helped me find the courage to go on."

The speakers rose one by one to praise Bob. Suddenly I heard myself being introduced: I had to give a speech. I wasn't prepared, what was I going to say? The others had already praised Bob to the high heavens, what could I add? A poem by James Henry Leigh Hunt popped into my head as I approached the podium. It nicely summed up my feelings about Bob, so I recited it for the people who had come to honor this good priest.

*Abou Ben Adhem (may his tribe increase!)*
*Awoke one night from a deep dream of peace,*
*And saw within the moonlight in his room,*
*Making it rich, and like a lily in bloom,*
*An Angel writing in a book of gold.*
*Exceeding peace had made Ben Adhem bold,*
*And to the presence in the room he said:*
*"What writest thou?" The vision raised its head,*
*And with a look made of all sweet accord*
*Answered, "The names of all those who love the Lord."*
*"And is mine one?" said Abou. "Nay, not so,"*
*Replied the Angel. Abou spoke more low,*
*But cheerily still; and said, "I pray thee, then,*
*Write me as one who loves his fellow-men."*
*The Angel wrote and vanished. The next night*
*It came again with a great wakening light,*
*And showed the names whom love of God had blessed,*
*And, lo! Ben Adhem's name led all the rest!*

"Love is indeed a blessing, both in heaven and here on earth," I said. "And Bob, who loves his fellow men, is certainly at the top of the list of the blessed."

---

Those who love the most are the winners in life.

---

## Love And The Immune System

*If I had the power of prophecy and*
*If I had the power to fathom all*
   *knowledge and wisdom and*
*If I had the faith that could move mountains*
*But if I didn't have love,*
*I'd be nothing.*

*I. Corinthians 13:2*

What blessing do you receive in exchange for loving your fellow man? Among many other things, good feelings that translate into good health.

We've already seen how enthusiasm and other positive "up" thoughts are converted into endorphins and other health-giving substances in the "E-Spot". Love — for yourself and others — is one of the strongest of these emotions that work their way through the "E-Spot" to give us vibrant health, physically, mentally and spiritually.

Love seems to have a special effect on the immune system, easily seen in babies. Babies have simple uncomplicated lives, requiring very little compared to adults. Babies must have food, clean diapers and so on or else they'll cry, become malnourished, develop diaper rashes and suffer the other indignities from being so helpless. As we all know, however, babies also require plenty of tender loving care; someone to pick them up, cuddle and kiss them, tell them that they are loved. Infants may not know the meaning of the words, but they understand absolutely the feeling of love.

Animal studies have shown that love (handling) influences a baby animal's weight gain, learning behavior, emotional reactions and the ability to respond to stress. One of the reasons that animals raised without the requisite love have a weakened response to stress is that their immune system is weak.

Look at Joannie. She felt the lack of love even as an infant, and she suffered for it. Her emotional reactions were certainly knocked askew by lack of love. Her immune system was weakened when I first saw her; the blood tests proved that. Who knows what shape it had been in until then? We do know that she suffered much more than usual from the childhood diseases and various infections. Was her mononucleosis also related to a compromised immune system? Absolutely.

We're all exposed to pretty much the same germs, although only a relatively small number of us become their victim. Why is that? Because those of us with strong immune systems shrug off the germs. On the other hand, those among us who have weak immune systems come down with whatever disease the germs are peddling. It doesn't matter why the immune system has been thrown for a loop. The cause can be physical or emotional. The germs don't care, they find a weakness and attack.

Joannie's lifelong disease (until she was cured) was lack of love. Lack of love from others. Lack of self-love. Lack of giving love. Everyone will agree that love is a kind of mother's milk for infants. Why, then, is it often so hard to get adults to acknowledge their own need for love? Yes, infants and adults are different. Mind and body change during the growth process. Still, love is a basic necessity, just like vitamins and minerals. Without love, the spirit turns cold and the immune system shrivels up.

---

Love is fuel for the flame of the spirit. Without love, the spirit dies.

---

## Fear And Guilt, Enemies Of Love

*Love alone dominates fear.*

*Zohar, Exod. 216a*

Fear is the antithesis of love. Fear is the reason so many of us suffer from lack of self-esteem. Fear is the reason we find it so difficult to love others.

Of what are we so afraid? If our self-esteem is low, we're frightened by most everything because our Comfort Zone is so small and our Tension Zone so near. So many things are painful. It only takes a thought or two to set our stomach a-twisting or our heart fluttering.

We're afraid to try and we're scared not to. We're

frightened of change but we're terrified by the status quo. We want more out of life but we're too timid to venture out of our shells. We can't let people in because they might hurt us. Worse yet, the example of loving living they set may make us painfully aware of how barren our life is.

Some fear is necessary. The fear engendered by the "fight or flight" response to stress can save our lives. But if we do occasionally need fear to get ourselves moving out of a dangerous situation, we do not need the constant state of low- to medium-grade fear I see in so many of my patients.

Often times you can tell that a person lives in their shell of fear and self-deprecation as soon as they open their mouth. You know how these people are: "Well, I don't like my job, but who knows if I could find another one?" Or, "No, he's not exactly a good husband, but I'm afraid to be alone," "I'm a loser," and "There are things I'd like to change, but I'm afraid to rock the boat." With their words, thoughts and actions, these people affirm to themselves that life is frightening, that so many things are too difficult to deal with, that they're unlucky or unworthy. Their negative thoughts are written into their mental blueprints for their subconscious to read and act on, converting unhappy thoughts to terrifying reality.

Then there's guilt, which is in some ways the "flip side" of fear. Fear is a future-tense feeling. We fear the future, we're afraid of things that will or will not happen. Guilt looks back to the past with an unhappy eye, taking in our failures, misdeeds and oversights.

We feel afraid; we don't want to look forward. We feel guilty; we can't bear to look back. Past and present are off limits but they're constantly on our mind, squeezing the present, choking off our air.

With fear threatening from one side and guilt from the other, where can we turn?

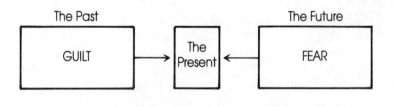

We feel guilt and fear because we have a poor self-image.
We allow these two terrible negations to shrink the boundaries
of our lives and bring our Tension Zones down on our heads.

## Love Conquers All

But if fear and guilt are the enemies of love, love is the
antidote. Build your self-esteem, your self-love. Open
yourself up to the love of others. Love living. Now you're
taking big steps toward conquering your fears and guilts.

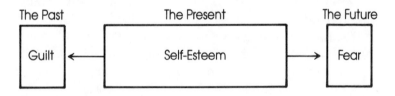

When you have goodly amounts of self-esteem, you can
admit your mistakes and failings without undue guilt. And
when you have self-love, you also have self-confidence.
With self-confidence by your side, the future is inviting
not fearful.

I'm not saying that love will banish fear and guilt forever
from your life. No, some fear and guilt will always be
present to remind us that we're only human. But love will
shrink fear and guilt down, push them away, put them into
perspective. When you have love, fear and guilt will not be
able to trap you in a very small present, afraid of both past
and future. Love unlocks the prison and sets you free.

---

Excessive fear and guilt are chains we wrap around ourselves. Generous amounts of love cut the chains by putting fear and guilt into perspective, allowing us to get on with life.

---

### I Eagerly Look Forward

Here's an affirmation to help you expand your self-esteem and self-love:

---

*I eagerly look forward to every new person, situation and challenge that comes my way. Every day is an exciting adventure. Armed with endless self-esteem and confidence, belief and enthusiasm, I'm conquering the world!*

---

## Giving Is Getting

Now that you've learned to love yourself, turn your love outward, onto others. Don't be afraid, as so many are, to love. Loving shouldn't be like reaching into your wallet to grudgingly give away some of your hard-earned money. Love is infinite. You can't possibly give away all you have because the more you give, the more you get from within and from others. Loving yourself and loving others feels good. You're happy when you're loving. That happiness rushes right to your "E-Spot" to trigger the release of endorphins and other beneficial biochemicals, translating your good mental feelings into a good physical feeling. The better you feel, the more positive your outlook on life and the greater your self-esteem. As your self-esteem grows, so does your ability to love others. Love is a positive feedback loop that need never end.

---

Love is a self-renewing resource; you can't possibly run out. It's only when you keep it to yourself or turn your back on it that the flame dies.

---

## How Do You Start Loving?

Begin by acknowledging that you have difficulty giving and receiving love. Tell yourself that you're going to work on this problem, and that the results will soon be evident. Now make a list of your good qualities:

1.

2.

3.

4.

5.

6.

7.

8.

Concentrate on the good. Don't worry if your good qualities are good enough or how they compare to other people's. Focus on the good that is within you. Now pick out a couple of people, write down at least one good thing about each of them:

Person 1:

Person 2:

Person 3:

Love is a strong fondness or enthusiasm for someone or something, so jot down some positive notes about things, situations, aspects of life you admire or enjoy as well:

Item 1:

Item 2:

Item 3:

Affirm your love for yourself, for other people and for aspects of life by concentrating on these good things you've just listed.

Keep the list of your good qualities in front of you at all times, like the Little Leaguers kept their affirmation card with them at all times. Begin each day by looking at your list of good qualities and review them often through the day. Read them to yourself and out loud. In so doing, you'll be affirming the goodness within you. Do the same with the other two lists you made, those describing the good qualities in other people and the positive aspects of daily life.

Seeing is believing, they say. Keep your lists in front of you all the time, like the Apple Power team did. See them with two eyes and with your mental eye. Write this goodness into your mental blueprints. Let the goodness expand your self-image and become a part of your outlook on life. You'll feel better about yourself, about others and about life. You'll be ready to love yourself and to love others.

## Reach Out And Touch Someone

Some patients wonder how to start, saying: "But, Dr. Fox, how do I start this whole love thing? I've got my lists, but I'm not used to loving anyone, or even thinking about love. I just can't walk up to people and say I love them."

Why not? Why can't you walk up to someone you love and say "I love you"? Because you're embarrassed? Embarrassment is fear, and fear is conquered by love.

In the Broadway show, *My Fair Lady*, Eliza Doolittle sings to her suitor: "Don't talk of love, show me!" I want you to show your love. Begin with yourself. After you've read this section, after you've thought and talked about it, after all the affirmations and promises, show yourself. How? By expressing love for someone else.

Pick any person you like: your spouse, lover, mother, father, brother, sister, son, daughter, friend, grandparent, whomever you prefer. Tell them you love them. If you can't use the word "love", say, "I appreciate all the good things you've done for me" or say, "Your friendship is very important to me" or "I really enjoy your company." If you can't even say that, you can certainly start loving them by offering a sincere compliment.

Be sure to look them in the eye when you tell them you love them. Touch them if you can. Hold their hand, put your hand on their shoulder, put your arm around their shoulder. Let them feel the fire of your spirit reaching out with love for them. The greater the warmth they feel, the more love you'll receive in return.

Give them some of your love with "the gesture". Touch your hand to your heart, then extend that same hand, fingers forward, to them. Make a present of your love to others. Tell them, "I'm giving you my love."

---

For every bit of love you give, you'll receive two in return: one from the one you gave to, the other from your own heart.

---

## The Healing Chemistry Of Love

*Love brings to life whatever is dead around us.*

F. Rosenzweig

Here's a beautiful story illustrating the healing chemistry of love.

It began when I arrived at the Los Angeles County Hospital to begin a Residency in Internal Medicine. Fresh from an Internship, I was looking forward to "commanding" my own group of Interns. Yesterday I was an Intern, a foot soldier in the army of medicine. Now I was a commander of the troops! And to back up my new-found status, I now wore the short white Resident's coat. (Interns wore the Intern's shirt, like Dr. Ben Casey did on television.) One day, one day soon, I told myself, I'll be wearing a doctor's long white coat!

That first day I arrived bright and early, eager to impress my Interns — and my superiors — with my wisdom and knowledge. Little did I know I would be taught something very important by one of my "troops". I had been briefed on my Interns, I knew who was considered sharp, who was thought so-so and who was called the "odd ball". As we made the rounds that first time, I asked them about themselves, about the hospital, their patients and so on. There were the usual introductions, shop-talk, complaints about the 36 hours on, 12 hours off schedule we all endured — the sort of chat that was probably going on between Interns and Residents all across the country.

Being new, I wasn't quite sure of my way around the giant hospital. As we headed toward a distant corner of the old building, the Interns suggested we go elsewhere to see patients. Ahead of us lay the surgical derelicts, they told me. I knew what they meant: those withered old people who have already had all the surgery they're going to have, and who haven't any exciting or exotic diseases for us to study. As a matter of fact, these people often have no clear-cut disease entity at all to excite the Interns, Residents, long-coated professors and department heads. No one ever goes there, my Interns told me. I knew they were right. Even today, these people are considered uninteresting by young doctors-in-training. My son, Eric, who just now completed his Residency in Internal Medicine, tells me that some doctors now call these surgical derelicts "gomers".

I decided to wander out that way anyway, just to see what was there. As we got to the "gomer" ward a young Intern rushed past us carrying a large tray of bottles of intravenous fluids. This was the "oddball", the others informed me. He's not very bright, they said. Through the haziness of the years I can remember him: stocky chest, light hair, glasses, his Intern's shirt open at the neck like Dr. Ben Casey on the television show. We caught up with him in the middle of this ward filled with frail, shrunken people so pale and lifeless, they seemed to be almost folded into their beds. They were the nameless benignly neglected ones.

"What are you doing?" I asked.

He saw my name tag and realized who I was. "Dr. Fox," he said with a calm, friendly chuckle, "I'm watering my flowers."

"What did you say?" I asked incredulously.

"Dr. Fox, I know you're originally from back east. I'm a Southern California boy. I grew up on the beaches and I know that if you see a dried up starfish and get it back into the water, it fills with fluid and comes back to life. Starfish and flowers need water. They are my flowers. I'm watering them," he said, his arm grandly sweeping around the room to indicate all the "gomers". This, by the way, was before air-conditioning was installed; it was easy for patients to become dehydrated in those hot wards.

"Okay," I said, "Keep me informed."

Just then I was paged and had to go take charge of a cardiopulmonary resuscitation in another part of the hospital. I spent the rest of the day going from one emergency or new patient to the next, and quickly forgot about the "oddball" Intern.

Several days later at the morning report, I asked the enthusiastic young Intern how the "watering" project was going. With a proud smile on his face he answered: "Come on down and see them."

I took my entire squad of Interns, medical students and nurses to the forgotten wards. They protested all the way, grumbling they had more interesting patients to see, more lectures to attend, more books to read: Who wants to waste time on a bunch of old people who don't have exotic diseases?

What a delightful surprise awaited us! The old people had sprung up like young flowers in bloom. Their eyes were bright. There were smiles on their faces. What made them so alive? It wasn't their medicine, for they had been receiving that for years. The intravenous fluids were certainly very important, but the special "medicine" that made the difference was the young Intern's love for his "flowers".

If he had given them the same intravenous fluid the way most of us would have done — grumbling, uninterested, eager to be elsewhere — some of these old people undoubtedly would have died. But this intern gave them something extra: love. Unlimited love. I don't know why; for some reason he loved his "flowers". That wonderful

love he spread so freely gave length to their lives and life
to their days. What did it matter that he could not rattle
off the names of 1,000 fascinating diseases or reel off
quote after quote from the medical authorities, like the
"bright" Interns could? He knew more about the true
essence of doctoring than most of us.

---

Love is the cure to many of the diseases afflicting us.

---

## Love Unconditionally

*Love your enemies, bless them that curse
you, do good to them that hate you, and pray
for them which despitefully use you and
persecute you.*

*Matthew 5:44*

Before giving you your affirmation for love of others,
let me add one more point, one that many of my patients
raise. What do you do when someone refuses to return
your love? Or even worse, they act as your enemy? Must
you love people like this?

Yes. Love them for your sake. If they refuse your
sincere offer of love, that's a problem they have to deal
with. Your job is to go on loving.

One of my patients is a beautiful 35-year-old woman,
athletic and well-educated, an executive with a large
medical corporation who travels around the country
trouble-shooting for the company. Although she meets
many eligible men, she's never married.

"I'm never going to love again," she announced to me
one day. "I've given out love, but those crummy men

never return it. I was always doing for them, but they never returned the favor."

Over the next couple of months she literally shut herself down, cutting herself off from love. I saw her several times during this period and as we talked, it became clear that she had always loved conditionally, had always expected something back. And she wasn't just satisfied with meeting nice men; she was looking for the bells and stars.

This woman made a common mistake, placing great expectations and heavy conditions upon her love. Naturally, she was disappointed.

Love freely. Love with no strings attached. Give love with nothing looked for in return. When you've learned to love like this, you'll be rewarded many times over with health, joy and love.

---

Give your love unconditionally, without expectations or demands. Love for the joy of loving.

---

### Love, Inward And Outward

Here's your affirmation for love:

---

*Whether looking inward to myself, or outward to the world, I see unlimited love. I definitely believe in the healing power of love, and I enthusiastically give it to everyone I meet. And every time I give my love away, I get twice as much back in return.*

---

Love is that thing which makes life worth living. It's the spark of the divine within you, the summation of all good things. Love gives meaning to your life, it lets you see the good in others and makes obvious the good in you. Love conquers all. Put its power to work for you.

# Forgive And Be Free

*Though your sins be as scarlet, they shall be
white as snow.*

*Isaiah 1:18*

A patient once asked me if it's easier to take care of
wealthy patients or people of more modest means.
Instead of answering the question directly, I pointed out
of the window near my desk that looks down over
northern Beverly Hills. "There are beautiful homes,
beautiful green trees and lawns, beautiful swimming
pools, beautiful cars and beautiful people, from West
Hollywood to Westwood. This is some of the most
expensive real estate in the world. I would say that the
people here are no happier than people anywhere. But
they do know one thing that poor people don't: They
know that money can't buy happiness."

"It is a great view," my patient agreed. "The green is
dazzling from up here. So is the green of their money,"
he laughed. "You know, I've been in almost all the big

houses down there, over the years. I've met the big
movie stars, the directors, the writers. I've seen them
come and go and you're right, there's a lot of unhappiness among the beautiful people. Why?"

"Probably for the same reasons people anywhere are
unhappy, no matter how much or little money they
have," I answered. "Lack of spirit, lack of love. I've also
seen among my rich patients many who are unable to
forgive and forget the harms they've suffered plus an
awful lot of guilt."

Then I told this man about one of my patients
(changing the details to conceal the identity). This
patient came to see me many years ago, when she was an
almost-great advertising executive, scrambling and
clawing her way to the top. Headaches, palpitations of
the heart, stomach pains, nervousness, anxiety and
irritability made her life almost unbearable, so an actor-
friend of hers told her to come see me.

I ushered the anxious woman into my office that first
day, to begin taking her personal and medical history.
When I offered her a seat, she declined, saying that she
preferred to stand. Before I got to my chair, she was
pacing back and forth, teeth clenched in anger, saying,
"I have a new account tomorrow, that's why I'm
nervous. Those bastards! They know I'm good but
they're making me make a presentation like I was some
kid starting out. If I could get them . . . My head is kill-
ing me. I have to sit down." And she sat down into the chair.

"Why have you come to see me?" I asked.

With a little smile she pulled a piece of paper from her
large purse and proceeded to read me a long and
detailed list of complaints, describing when and where
each one hit, what it felt like, how long it lasted and so
on. As she recited, I furiously scribbled notes on her
medical history form. She also showed me 13 or 14
bottles of medicine prescribed for her by various
physicians. It took so long to discuss and copy down this
information that we ran past the allotted time, so I asked
her to come back the following week.

The next week she dragged herself into my office, dropped her jacket and purse and slumped into a chair. She looked too exhausted to move. In just a moment, however, she was up on her feet, hands in front of her as if she were holding a gun. "If I had a machine gun I'd kill them. They didn't give me the job. I could kill those bastards!" she said.

I hadn't seen anyone that angry in a long time. And all because they wouldn't give her the account? This woman was obviously over-reacting. When she calmed down a bit, I told her that I had been reviewing the history form she had filled out the previous week, and noticed that she'd left blank the parts which have to do with her family.

"How old is your mother?" I asked. "Is she alive? How's her health?"

"I don't want to talk about my mother," she answered brusquely.

I was a little startled by her attitude but continued. "Well, how about your father?"

"I don't want to talk about my father," she said icily.

"Your brothers and sisters?"

"I don't want to talk about them, either. I haven't seen them for years. I came here to find out why I'm sick, not talk about my family."

We sat quietly for a moment. Then I said, "We haven't finished your history or even begun the physical examination or tests, but I'll bet your family has something to do with why you're sick."

She looked at me, eyes filled with anger. "Do you know what my mother did to me?! I haven't spoken to her in ten years because of the things she did, and I don't care if I never speak to her again! Or any of them!"

I thought for several seconds, then turned to her and said quietly, "I have an answer to many of your problems."

She brightened up, smiled and leaned forward in her chair. "Great. What is it?"

"Call your mother and forgive her."

"What?!" she jumped to her feet. "What?" And she picked up her purse, which was big and heavy, and

swung it at my head like an executioner swinging the ax.
Luckily I caught it, inches from my face.

Shouting that I was obviously a fraud, she kicked her
chair and yanked open the door.

That's when I very firmly said: "Sit down!"

She must have been startled, because she came back
and sat down. But only for a moment. Then she was
back on her feet, scowling, heading out the door.
Another firm "sit down" got her back in the chair and I
talked to her — at her — for at least 20 minutes, telling
her what happens when you refuse to forgive someone,
how it rips you up inside, sending distress calls to the
"surface" with what we call disease.

## Let Go Of Your Anger

If you're angry at someone, if you haven't forgiven
them, you're hanging onto rage, embarrassment, humiliation, pain, frustration and other very negative feelings.
Allowing these emotions to fester in the mind results in
the constant, inappropriate production of body chemicals that are dangerous when present in the wrong
proportions. Embracing anger, for example, prompts
the manufacture of high-voltage chemicals in the body,
such as adrenaline, noradrenaline, ACTH and cortisone.
These and other chemicals are needed by the body when
we have to physically fight or run for our lives. But if
there's no one to punch and no where to run, a body full
of these substances is a rapidly ticking time bomb.

With overproduction of adrenaline, for example,
comes contractions of the muscles in the neck and head.
This leads to tension-vascular headaches. Unnecessary
secretion of certain chemicals in the nerve tissue and in
other parts of the body causes the heart to pound like a
sledgehammer in your chest and to beat irregularly.
Substances produced by a failure to forgive also cause
the pains in the stomach we doctors call erosive gastritis
or peptic ulcer of the duodenum or stomach or esopha-

gitis. And those episodes of diarrhea we say are related to the irritable bowel syndome. They're really related to these very same chemicals.

This woman couldn't forgive. Neither could she rid herself of all her ills.

---

"Unforgiveness" is a terrible disease that attacks you, not the person you're mad at.

---

## Forgiveness Is A Gift To Yourself

"Do you know what my mother did to me!?" the advertising executive demanded when I suggested she forgive her mother. "Do you have any idea?"

"No, and it's not important. Call her up and forgive her."

"Never!"

She was determined to hold on to her anger! We went back and forth, neither willing to budge. Finally she said: "Why should I give her the satisfaction of being forgiven, when I'm the one who was hurt?"

"Because you're the one who is suffering. Besides, you're not forgiving her for her sake — you're forgiving her for your sake." She looked surprised, and I continued:

"*Forgiveness is a gift to yourself.* Forgiveness allows your body to turn down the manufacture of those chemicals which are tearing you apart, body and soul. You're not really suffering from gastric this or vascular that. Your real disease is 'unforgiveness', one of the great diseases of our time. The other doctors have been treating your head, your heart, your stomach, your colon and your anxiety. It hasn't helped much, has it?" She shook her head. "I want you to treat yourself by throwing away your hatred.

"You told me you've already had two disastrous marriages and nasty divorces, plus a succession of men in and out of your life. You said you're sick all the time. You told me you're unhappy. Now I'm telling you to end it all by forgiving your mother for whatever she's done — I don't care what it is. The bottom line is this: Forgive, and there's a good chance you'll get rid of your problems and move on with life. Or hold on to your anger — and your unhappiness and your headaches and your palpitations and your stomach pains and your anxiety and your bag full of medicines."

She thought about what I said for a while, then asked: "Just saying I forgive her will take care of everything?"

"Not everything," I answered, "and you can't just say it. You have to *feel* it, mean it. Saying it and meaning it are the first steps. We might find other problems, but forgiving her is a good first step."

"I'll do it," she said. "What do I have to do?"

"Call your mother — right now — and forgive her. Do you remember the number?"

She nodded. "Do I have to see her?"

"Not if you don't want to."

"She's going to say something nasty to me."

"That's her problem. Just tell her you forgive her. At least three times, if you can."

"Ok, but I'll have to practice first."

That seemed fair. After all, she hadn't seen or spoken to her mother for ten years. "Can I practice in here alone for 15 minutes?" she wanted to know.

I agreed, and stepped out into the hall. Through the closed door I heard her voice: "Mother, I forgive you. Mother, I forgive you." It sounded phony and forced. I went to the waiting room to talk with another patient. Fifteen minutes later I walked back to my office. In the hallway, as I opened the door, I heard her again: "Mother, I forgive you. Mother, I forgive you." Now she was saying it with sincerity and humility. I felt she was ready. She agreed.

"I'll go home and call her," she said.

"No. I want you to call her right now. Use my phone."

Hesistantly she dialed the numbers, motioning for me to stay. After a brief pause she said, very slowly: "Mother, I forgive you." There was a pause, then she repeated the words: "Mother, I forgive you." After another pause she said it again, clear and strong: "Mother, I forgive you." Then I heard nothing for quite some time, and I wondered what her mother was saying. Was the mother really an evil woman? Was she berating her daughter? Was she heaping guilt on the daughter for walking out on her ten years ago?

Finally, I smiled in relief as the executive spoke in a relaxed voice, asking about her father and brothers, old friends and neighbors. Before saying goodbye, the executive invited her mother to come visit her at her home in Malibu.

She hugged me as she left the office, saying, "I don't know if it will last, but I feel so good now!"

Three days later she brought her mother to meet me, saying with a smile, "Mother, this is Dr. Fox. He's the one who brought us together, and I think he saved my life."

Well, I don't know about saving her life, but I can tell you that her problems cleared up within a few weeks. The headaches, the palpitations, stomach pains, irritability, anxiety and the nervousness vanished when she let go of her anger. I don't see her as often anymore — there's really no need except for the routine examinations.

You can see why I like practicing this "new" kind of medicine — it works so well because it rids the mind of the negative emotions that drag us down into disease and depression, allowing our natural defenses to keep us healthy and happy.

> Forgiveness of others is a gift to ourself, a healing medicine for many of our physical and emotional ills.

## Who Should You Forgive?

Forgive everyone who has ever harmed you. Even the crook that broke into your house and stole all your jewelry? Yes. The gossip who publically embarrassed you? Yes. The fraud who cheated you out of all your money? Yes.

"Come on, Dr. Fox," some might say. "You'll have me bending over backward to kiss people who hurt me."

You don't have to reward the people who harmed you. You don't have to love them, or even like them. You certainly don't have to thank them for hurting you. All you have to do is forgive them. It's so simple . . . and so important.

> Forgiveness has nothing to do with *them*, but everything to do with *you*. Forgiveness is a way of making sure you're not harboring any of the destructive feelings that sap your health and happiness.

## Double-edged Forgiveness

Forgiveness is a glorious feeling that sets you free. But even if you already have the feeling of forgiveness inside of you, you must still say the words "I forgive you" out loud. That is vital. The words are in a sense an affirmation with a hidden meaning. When you say, "I forgive you," you're communicating with the other person. You're also speaking to yourself, saying, "Right here and now I banish the negative feelings I have toward this person. I am expelling the anger, rage, frustration, hostility, humiliation, pain and so forth from my mind and body. I'm doing this so I can get on with my life."

---

Forgiveness instructs your subconscious to banish negative feelings from your mind. When you say, "I forgive you" to someone, you're also saying, "I want to be healthy" to yourself.

---

## How Do You Forgive?

Forgive with all your heart. Remember, the words have two messages to convey, one to the person you forgive, and another, much more important, to yourself. Simply mouthing the words is not enough. You may fool the person you're forgiving, but you won't deceive yourself. So act, walk, talk, think and behave as if you truly forgive — as if you're already forgiven.

The best way to forgive is to forgive in person, out loud. It's the best way because it's the hardest way. If you can gather the courage, determination and sincerity to forgive in person, your words will have more meaning and effect.

---

Forgive in person, forgive over the phone, forgive by mail, if you must. However it must be done, forgive.

---

## Forgiving The Dead

One man said that he agreed he should forgive his father, who he still hated for squeezing him out of the family business 20 years ago. "But", he explained, "I have a problem that prevents me from apologizing to Dad. He's dead and buried."

I've seen many patients who are nourishing anger at their deceased parents. One 70-year-old man was still angry at his father for not allowing him to study opera 50 years ago. A 65-year-old man still complained about his disapproving mother: "If I got a B+, she asked why it wasn't an A. Nothing I could do was good enough for her." (Fortunately, my own mother was much less demanding. When I pulled my grade in woodshop up to a D, she was thrilled.)

One of the nice things about forgiveness is that the other person doesn't have to hear you say you forgive them in order for it to work — for you to begin feeling better immediately. So if the person you need to forgive has passed away, you can still forgive them. Go down to the cemetery, stand over their grave and tell him or her that they are forgiven. Cemeteries are great places to forgive someone who has died — the best place, in fact. It doesn't matter that the deceased can't hear you, or that they'll never know you forgave them. You forgave. That's good enough.

---

Death of the person you're angry at does not diminish your need to forgive — or the benefits of forgiveness. Graveside forgiveness is proper and effective.

---

## Seventy Times Seven

The story about the advertising executive had a happy ending. Her mother was so glad to hear from her daughter, she never dared to do any of the terrible things she used to do (whatever they were). But suppose you forgive some-one, only to find that they hurt you again? And again and again? Or what if they refuse to accept your forgiveness?

How many times should you — can you — forgive someone? Where do you draw the line? Nowhere. Don't draw any line, don't set any limits. Forgive them now and forever. In the Scriptures it is written that we should forgive them seventy times seven times: I say forgive seventy times seven thousand times, if need be. Don't even keep tally. The key is to forgive, freely and forever. Why? Because "unforgiveness" is a terrible scourge that can ruin you, emotionally, spiritually and physically.

---

It's better to forgive ten thousand hurts than to allow one bit of anger to poison your mind and body.

---

## Failure To Forgive Yourself

*Every guilty person is his own hangman.*

*Seneca*

Failure to forgive is an endemic health problem. And so is guilt, which is failure to forgive with a special twist. With guilt, instead of remembering all the terrible things someone has done to you, you're clinging to memories of the things you've done wrong. The object of your negative feelings is different, but the methods and results are the same.

Let me tell you about a woman who didn't forgive herself.

I was talking on the telephone in my office when my nurse walked in and said, "I think you'd better see Mrs. Green."

"She's just here for a blood test. Is there a problem?"

"She looks terrible. You should see her."

I went into the patient examining room to find Mrs. Green staring down through the large window at Santa Monica Boulevard, seven stories below.

"Counting cars?" I asked. Tearfully she told me that her mother had suffered a stroke and was in the hospital, in a coma. I had met her mother once before, an opinionated woman who expected big things from her daughter. Unfortunately, Mrs. Green had not lived up to her mother's expectations. To put it mildly, her life was a mess. Mrs. Green and I had spoken about this several times, discussing changes she might want to make.

In between sobs, Mrs. Green told me she had finally taken my advice and had gone to visit her mother in the rest home, only to find she'd had a stroke and had been rushed to the hospital.

"She may die. She was so difficult, especially after my divorce. I feel so bad. I feel so guilty because I don't like her."

And she cried on my shoulder, sobbing, "I love her. I love her and I feel so bad. She's been sick for years but I never did anything. What should I do?"

"Forgive her," I said. "The only way for you to get better is to forgive your mother."

"How? She's in a coma. She may die without waking up."

"It's not as important that she hear you say it, as it is that you say it. And feel it. Forgive her. Then forgive yourself. Get rid of your guilt by forgiving yourself. It doesn't matter whose fault it was. You can't carry around guilt. It only makes you sick. Heal the wounds with forgiveness, and start all over again."

I drew the little squares to show how guilt and fear squash love and life, then told her to look in the mirror every morning, point her finger at herself and say:

*For any and all wrongs she has done to me, I forgive my mother. Right here and now with all my heart and soul, I forgive her. Freely and without hesitation, I throw away all my anger and replace it with forgiveness.*

*And for any and all wrongs I have done to her, I forgive myself. Right here and now, with all my heart and soul, I forgive myself. Freely and without hesitation I throw away all my guilt and replace it with determination to start anew.*

*In forgiving myself, my mother and anyone else who might have wronged me, I free myself now from the shackles of anger and guilt. I am allowing myself to be what I want to be, to do what I want to do and to have what I want to have.*

Mrs. Green brightened up immediately, asking me to write that affirmation down. "I'll go right to her bedside and say it," she promised. And she did.

The power of forgiveness is amazing. A few simple words, coupled with strong belief, can turn your life around.

## Numbed By Guilt

Guilt is every bit as terrible and dangerous as failure to forgive another person can be. Let me tell you about one woman whose guilt was converted into crippling physical symptoms.

Late one Sunday night some 20 years ago, I received a call to come to the hospital and see a patient at the request of her general practitioner. She was to be operated on by a neurosurgeon the next day, and her doctor wanted me to make sure her heart was strong enough to withstand the stress of surgery.

It was late. I was tired, but the doctor had been a student of mine, so I went to the hospital. Going into the woman's hospital room, I ran into the neurosurgeon. When he asked me why I was there, I told him I was going to check the woman's heart in preparation for surgery. "Well," he said, "I didn't ask for you. I don't need you." I told him I was sorry, but her doctor wanted me to check her out. Without another word the neurosurgeon left.

Inside the patient's room, I saw a 37-year-old woman lying in bed, smoking a cigarette. I introduced myself and took a lengthy and careful history. She told me she'd begun to experience weakness of her right foot several weeks ago. She'd first noticed the problem when she was driving. The weakness had progressed until she was unable to drive safely. Then it became associated with weakness of her right hand, and finally, both her right foot and hand were now paralyzed and numb.

The examination progressed normally until I got to the neurologic part. She felt nothing when I pushed a pin into the skin of the sole of her right foot. Neither did she blink an eye when I pushed the pin into her right hand. What interested me was not that she felt no pain, but that she seemed completely indifferent to her loss of feeling — *la belle indifference*, as the textbooks say. Her complete lack of concern suggested that she was suffering from a stress, not a neurologic (nerve) problem. This might be a conversion reaction, in which emotional distress is converted into physical symptoms.

I got on the telephone and tracked down her general practitioner through his exchange. He was having dinner at Scandia's restaurant on the Sunset Strip. "Can I administer truth serum to your patient?" I asked. He agreed, saying he would be pleased if I could save her from surgery.

Taking a nurse with me, I slowly administered a small amount of the sedative sodium pentothal ("truth serum") to the woman, talking with her when she was in a half-awake, half-unconscious state.

As we spoke about the day she first experienced weakness of her foot, she slowly and hesitantly told me that she had just seen her father for the first time in 15 years on that day. He looked shabby, old and ill. She couldn't bear to be with him long because she felt so guilty for abandoning him 15 years before when he needed her help. After giving him some money, she'd sent him away, then got into her car and drove up and down the coast highway for hours. That's when she first noticed the weakness in her right foot.

"Give me that pin in your hat," I said to the nurse. Surprised at my strange request, she pulled the long, thin hat pin out of her peaked, highly starched nurses' cap. I quickly drove the sharp pin into the patient's right foot.

She pulled her whole leg back, face filled with surprise and pain. Then I stuck the pin into her right hand. She jerked her hand away. The nurse and I knew she was not paralyzed. This was a conversion reaction. She had transformed her guilt over her father into symptoms of paralysis. I called her doctor at the restaurant. He was ecstatic to hear she would not require surgery and asked me to write orders on the patient's chart, canceling the surgery.

(When I came back to see her the next day, I noticed that the neurosurgeon who had been so unpleasant to me had written on the patient's chart that he was pleased that unnecessary surgery had been avoided. It takes a big man to admit that he had overlooked one possible explanation for the woman's problem. He and I later became good friends.)

It took a while, but the woman's general practitioner, whom she trusted, worked with her in the hospital, explaining how her emotional distress was converted into the paralysis and numbness. Within a week she was able to walk out of the hospital. She took the lesson she learned to heart, seeking out her father, resolving her feelings of guilt and forgiving herself.

---

Guilt is failure to forgive yourself. Like failure to forgive others, guilt is a destructive feeling.

---

## When Bad Memory Is A Good Thing

*Happiness? That's nothing more than health and a poor memory.*

*Albert Schweitzer*

Let me go on record as favoring bad memories — selectively bad memories, that is. I propose that we all undertake to forget the wrongs we have suffered, whether they be by our own hand or by the hands of others. Let's forget all about them.

Now, when I tell you to forget the wrongs you've suffered, I really mean that you should banish the memory of the bad feelings associated with the wrongs, but not necessarily the facts.

Let's say someone swindled you out of all your money: What should you do? Forget your justifiable anger and indignation. Remember the facts, so you won't be swindled the same way again. But forget the feeling.

---

Being wronged is often less terrible than the constant memory of the wrong. Forgive and forget.

---

## Divide And Bury

*I've a grand memory for forgetting.*

### Robert Louis Stevenson

One patient got angry when I told him to forget the wrongs done to him. He got red in the face and shouted — yes, shouted — at me: "I'm a businessman, Dr. Fox. I'm realistic. Realistically, you can't forget it when someone hurts you. I don't care how Pollyanna you are. You can't and that's that!"

Forgetting the hurt is a difficult task. But you must or the hurt will torture you all the way to the grave. How do you do it? Well, forgetfulness begins with division. Divide the feelings from the facts. Mentally put the facts in one pile, the feelings in another. Take a look at the pile of feelings with your mind's eye — it's awfully big, isn't it? How can you possibly deal with all those feelings? Don't deal with them — dump them!

With your mind's eye, see a big bulldozer drive up to the pile of bad feelings and push it right over the side of a cliff. Watch the bad feelings as they fall down, down, down . . . it's a long way down . . . so far down, you can't see the bottom. Watch that pile of bad feelings falling further and further down until it's so small you can't see it anymore. You can't see the feelings, and you can't feel them. They're gone forever. Imagine this little scene in your mind several times, until the feelings really are gone. It will take a while to forget the feelings, so run this visualization over and over in your head. How many times? As many times as it takes.

Meanwhile turn your mind's eye to the pile of facts. Examine them. Ask yourself if it's really important for you to remember these facts. Will they save you from being harmed in the future? If not, have the bulldozer push them over the cliff. But if you think you should save these facts for future reference, send them to the laundry of your mind for a good cleaning. Make sure any

lingering emotions or feelings are washed off the facts.
Then file them away in your mind for future reference.

---

A wrong remembered is a pain relived. A wrong forgotten
is a pain no longer felt.

---

## Sin

*To err is human, to forgive divine.*

*Alexander Pope*

I told the story of the woman who became paralyzed
by her guilt to another woman I met while speaking to a
group of executives. She got very upset, saying that the
woman had committed a terrible sin by abandoning her
elderly sick father.

"He wasn't able to take care of himself. He could have
died because of her," she insisted. "What she did was a
sin. I don't think that kind of sin can be forgiven."

That's a pretty straight and narrow attitude to take.
After all, what is sin? Our word "sin" comes from the
Greek for "to miss the mark". Not "to be horrible", not
"to be the most despicable person there ever was", but
simply, "to miss the mark".

Who among us always hits the mark? Who is without
sin? Who can cast the first stone? Only the dead can
confidently say they will never sin again. The rest of us
can only do our best.

I don't care what you've done to someone else or to
yourself. I don't care what your "sin" is. Don't torture
yourself with guilt. Make amends, apologize, pay them
back, go to jail if you have to, but don't condemn
yourself to a lifetime of self-torture.

The same goes for forgiveness of others. Forgive them here and now. Forgive for your sake, if not theirs. You can demand restitution or testify against them in court in order to see justice done or to recover what is rightfully yours. But forgive them now and forever. Forgive them, else you condemn yourself to a mind filled with hate, a body filled with dangerous high-voltage chemicals and a lifetime of disease and unhappiness.

In the Scriptures it says, "Let not sin therefore reign in your mortal body . . ." (Romans 6:12). Don't let missing the mark warp your mind and body. Don't let the failure to forgive — yourself or others — destroy your health and happiness. Decide here and now that you will forgive the sins committed against you, as well as the sins you commit.

---

The target that is perfection is far away and small, very hard to hit. We're all going to miss the mark occasionally. When that happens, forgive yourself and try again.

---

## Don't Wait For God To Forgive You — Forgive Yourself

Steve, my patient and friend, told me about a man named John he had met recently.

"John's a bum and an alcoholic. Can you help him?" Steve asked me. "I'll take care of his bill."

"Is he a friend of yours?" I asked

"No. I just met him a while ago," Steve answered.

"Why are you going to pay what could be a very expensive bill for someone you barely know?" I asked curiously.

"There's something about him that tells me he's a good man. And he needs your help."

A few weeks later John came to my office. He was

quite a contrast to the usually well-dressed, nicely groomed people whom I see in my Beverly Hills office. Dirty, wearing ill-fitting clothes, he had unkempt hair, a shaggy beard, alcohol on his breath and bloodshot eyes. He must have made quite an impression on my patients, many who shop on fashionable Rodeo Drive, just a few blocks away. John was 38 years old, although he looked much older, and carried himself like a worn-out old man who has given up on life.

Eyes to the ground, he limply shook my hand and listlessly said: "Steve told me to come here." Then he looked me right in the eye. I could see strength come into his eyes, for just a quick moment, as he said defiantly, "You're supposed to help me."

I took the usual personal and medical history, performed a thorough physical examination, blood and other tests. Like most alcoholics, he was malnourished. I spoke to him about nutrition, vitamins and minerals, explaining how poor diet and alcohol combine to knock the body and immune system off balance. Additionally, I pointed out, alcohol reduces the flow of blood to the frontal lobes of the brain, which can result in all sorts of problems.

Even as we spoke, however, I knew that all the facts and figures I could give him about nutrition, alcohol, the liver, the brain and what have you, would make absolutely no difference in this man's life. Yes, he intellectually understood what I was saying, for here was clearly an intelligent, well-educated person. My words made an impression on his rational, thinking brain, but they failed to touch his spirit. Unless I could touch his spirit he would be back on the street, bottle in hand, sleeping in the gutters and alleys.

"What happened to you?" I asked. "What turned an obviously bright, capable person into the depressed drunkard sitting in front of me?"

He wouldn't say. But as we continued talking about belief, enthusiasm, motivation and the spirit, he perked up quite a bit. Before he left, he promised me he would

eat better, take the vitamins and minerals I prescribed
and cut back on the alcohol.

Steve looked after John, and told me that John's attitude
toward life had improved, that he was hardly drinking at
all and was taking better care of himself. All went well for
several weeks, until John showed up at my office reeking
of alcohol, tears streaming down his cheeks.

"I don't know why I started drinking again, Dr. Fox,"
he cried. "I'm so ashamed."

I thought for a while, then told him that he was hiding
something from me, something he felt very guilty about.
Although he denied it, I persisted until he finally said,
"What I did is so terrible I can't tell you."

"Try me," I answered.

Hesitantly he unfolded the story. He had been a
minister in a church in Texas, with a wife and a three-
year-old daughter. One misguided night, he went to bed
with a woman in his congregation. They were caught,
and the unfortunate man lost his wife and daughter, as
well as his position as minister. For five years he
wandered around the country, trying to drink himself to
death, until he made his way to Los Angeles and was
befriended by Steve.

"I don't ever remember coming here," he sobbed. "I
don't know how I got here. See how terrible I am, Dr.
Fox? What I did was so terrible that God will never
forgive me."

"That's right," I said, excited, leaning forward in my
chair. *God will never forgive you — because God never
condemned you!* You condemned yourself! God's not
punishing you — you're punishing yourself with your
guilt. I read in the paper that the governor has pardoned
a man who served ten years in jail for committing some
terrible crime. Isn't it time for you to pardon yourself,
and let yourself out of the mental jail with bars of guilt
you put yourself in?"

"Pardon myself?" he said.

"Yes!" I urged. "You're the only one who can free you.
All right. You made a mistake. You've been punished.

Now it's time to get on with your life. Pardon yourself here and now."

It took more talk, but he agreed to forgive and free himself. We worked out an affirmation to get him started. I told him to say it over and over through the day, and especially at night:

---

*At this very moment and forever, by the virtue of God within me, I hereby freely, willingly and without hesitation forgive myself for any wrongs committed in the past. I see and visualize myself free of guilt and fear. I let loose of all guilt and fear in my life. I let it go and I feel good. Now I am free to do what I have to do, have what I have to have and to be what I have to be.*

---

A spiritual man, the minister took the affirmation to heart, especially the words "by the virtue of God within me". He etched the affirmation into his mind, repeated it over and over, made it part of his mental makeup.

"With the help of that affirmation, and with the help of God within me, I'm going to come out of this, Dr. Fox," he promised me. And he did. Soon he had joined Alcoholics Anonymous and found a job as a secretary for an organization of churches. It was obvious to his employers that he had special talents, as well as a feeling for the downtrodden. Soon he was asked to head up the group's special counseling unit.

"That affirmation turned my life around, Dr. Fox," he told me many months later. "I tell my clients what you told me — enough is enough. You can't punish yourself forever. Everyone I counsel is given that same affirmation that saved my life. I tell them it's a special prayer that's always answered."

### I See Forgiveness

Everyday, morning, noon and night, I want you to say this affirmation for forgiveness and guilt. Even if you think already you've forgiven everyone, I want you to say it. Why? Because unforgiveness and guilt are terrible diseases that must be stamped out. If you've neglected to forgive someone, or to forgive yourself, this affirmation will help immensely. If you aren't withholding forgiveness, think of the affirmation as a vaccine to protect you in the future.

---

*Today, right here and now, I freely forgive anyone who may have wronged me in word or deed. Today, right here and now, I forgive myself for any wrongs I have committed. Now I am wonderfully free to become the person I want to be and to have the successful, happy and healthy life I so richly deserve.*

*I see forgiveness everywhere because I see it in myself.*

---

Say this affirmation for forgiveness over and over again, all day long, out loud and to yourself. You can also use the affirmations for guilt the woman and the minister used. Forgiveness is a vital virtue: Make sure you have plenty of it.

# Never Give Up!

*Courage mounteth with occasion.*

*Shakespeare: King John*

And now we come to perseverance, the final of the five virtues. What is perseverance? Perseverance is persistence in the face of adversity, the determination to never give in. No matter the odds or costs, you're going to do it! It's the last of the five virtues, not because it is any less important, but because the art of unconquerable perseverance requires mastery of the first four virtues. Let's take a detailed look at perseverance.

First, perseverance is belief. To persevere, you must believe in yourself. You *must* have the unshakable conviction that you deserve to succeed.

Second, perseverance is self-love. To persevere, you must have the self-confidence (self-love) necessary to withstand any number of defeats and turndowns. You *must* know that you're a worthy person, despite your temporary lack of success.

Third, perseverance is forgiveness. To persevere, you must be able to forgive yourself your momentary failure to reach the goal, and forgive others their inability to realize that they should be helping you. Unconditionally forgive them for turning you down.

Finally, perseverance is enthusiasm. Enthusiasm is essential to perseverance. You *must* have plentiful supplies of enthusiasm in order to put yourself whole-heartedly to the task once again, no matter how many times success has eluded you.

When you put it all together — belief, self-love, forgiveness and enthusiasm — you have perseverance. You have the courage, determination and patience to never give in.

---

Grasp firmly onto enthusiasm, belief, love and forgiveness:
Now you have the courage to succeed in spite of any odds.

---

Let's look at how perseverance helped some people, and see what lessons we can draw for our own lives.

### Never Give In!

*By perseverance the snail reached the ark.*

*Charles Haddon Spurgeon*

Many years ago I was the youngest sales representative employed by a large pharmaceutical firm. This was when I was in medical school, and in perpetual need of money for tuition, rent and food for my wife and kids. I had wrangled the job by brashly promising the boss I could get in to see the doctors, who would not see their regular reps, because I was a medical student. I implied there was some sort of medical fraternity and that I was a member.

Well, I was given the list of "hard-to-see" doctors, and quickly found out why they were on the list: Getting in to see them was like pulling teeth.

One day I was having lunch with the other reps. They asked which doctors I planned to see today. I told them Dr. Dobson was first on my list.

"Forget it, Kid," they said. "You'll never get in to see him. He's a mean old cuss who doesn't see reps."

"Well," I said, "I promised the boss I would see everybody on my list and that's exactly what I'm going to do today."

They laughed. One of them said: "You'll never get in. In all the years I've been at this, I've never been able to see him. If he won't let me in, he's not going to let you in. He only deals with the rep from one small company. You won't get in."

I took that as a challenge. I was going to get in, and that's all there was to it. But they were right: Dr. Dobson did not let me in the door. After climbing the stairs to the old building that housed his office and knocking on the door, I heard a voice from within: "Who's there?"

"I'm Arnold Fox, a pharmaceutical rep."

"Go away. I don't see reps."

He sounded so insistent that I left. The following week I again knocked on his door, and was again told to go away. This went on for four weeks.

On the fifth week he opened the door a crack and peered out at me. "Sonny," he said, "I've been buying my pharmaceuticals for over 40 years from the same company, and I'm not about to change now. I'm almost retired and I'm hardly seeing any patients anymore. Don't waste your time."

I answered, "I'll be back to see you every week because I promised the company I'd tell you about our products."

He closed the door and I left. I hadn't got in the door yet, hadn't even got my foot in. But at least the door had opened, if only a crack.

The following week I was back again. This time he opened the door wide. He was quite an elderly man, tall and thin, slouching slightly forward. "My, you are a persistent young man. I admire persistence. Come in."

He ushered me into his old office, past dusty stacks of journals and papers, and we sat down at a desk piled high with books and ancient instruments. Then he asked, "Sonny, what would have happened if I hadn't seen you today?"

"I'd be back next week."

"Weren't you upset that I didn't see you?"

"No. I didn't take it personally."

"I like that. Open up your sample case and let me see what I can buy from you."

I opened up my big black sample case and watched as he slowly moved his finger up and down the rows of ampules and vials of medicine, one by one, reading each label carefully. After what seemed like an eternity he selected a single medicine: "I'll take one vial. Mail it to me."

"Fine." I quickly calculated my commission on the single vial: about enough for a hamburger and a Coke. But I was pleased that I had done what they said could not be done, and sold him something.

As I was packing up my sample case he said: "I really like your persistence. I can't buy much from you, but let me call one of my ex-students. He has a big clinic. He could buy a lot."

He dialed the number and I heard him say: "Jim, I've got a bright young medical student in my office. He's very persistent and I want you to help him. I'm going to send him right over."

The old doctor gave me an address and sent me on my way. Soon I was seated in Dr. Lesser's office at a nearby clinic. Dr. Lesser was a short, chubby, bald and bubbling man who told me that old Dr. Dobson was the best teacher he had ever had. "That old man was good to me, so I'm going to repay him by being good to you. Get your order pad out and start writing, Kid."

In a few minutes time, Dr. Lesser had ordered more pharmaceuticals than I had sold in months. Not only that, he called other doctors and insisted that they see me as well. Many of them bought from me. I made the money I always desperately needed during those difficult school days.

And there was another reward to my perseverance: I became a friend of old Doctor Dobson. He took me out to the country house where he kept a dozen antique cars. I got to meet many of the celebrities involved with the antique car club and made many new friends.

Most of all, this experience taught me the importance of perseverance. Any one of my fellow pharmaceutical reps could have got in to see Dr. Dobson. All they had to do was knock on his door enough times. Sure, I was lucky to stumble upon Dr. Dobson, and be sent to Dr. Lesser and the others. But anyone else could have been just as lucky, had they kept knocking.

Throughout life you'll find many doors barring your way. Keep knocking. The worst that can happen is they say "no".

---

Never give in. The more turndowns you've had, the greater the odds that the next door you knock on will be the winner.

---

## Persevering Positivity

*Be strong and of good courage; be not afraid, neither be thou dismayed . . .*

*Joshua*

"Dr. Fox, am I ever going to get better?" Before I could reply, this beautiful woman answered her own questions: "I'm never going to get better. I know it."

Alexis had been ill, in and out of hospitals and doctors' offices for some ten years, a decade that saw her submit to multiple surgeries and try countless different medications. But the "giant waves" of illness, as she called them, kept coming back. We doctors had been unable to find an organic cause for the problem.

Lexy had an interesting career. She was the voice of many characters on TV and radio shows and commercials. She often said her job was the only thing that kept her going. One night, however, she gave up. In her mind's eye she could see no hope, so she took an overdose of sedatives. I was called to the emergency department of the hospital they brought her to. Luckily, we were able to revive her. The next day we spoke at length about what had happened.

"Oh, Dr. Fox, I'm so sorry I caused you so much trouble, but I've given up. I know I'll never get better. I can't face it anymore; I haven't the courage. In fact, I gave up a long time ago."

I listened to her, acknowledging her problems and fears. Although some doctors considered her a crank, I believed she was genuinely distressed. Plus I had learned by this time in my career that listening to a patient, really listening to them, is a powerful medicine. When she was all talked out, I said:

"Lexy, I wish I could tell you that I had the solution to your problems. I wish I could wave my magic wand and make things better, but I can't. All I can tell you is that there's a beginning, middle and end to every problem. Many people give up too soon, not realizing that they're in the middle, or maybe almost to the end of their problem.

"With most of our difficulties, a major part of the answer is stick-to-it-ness, courage. General George Patton, one of my favorite heroes, said that courage is hanging on for another five minutes."

"How can I keep holding on? Where can I find the courage?"

"Well, lets look at your positive qualities. You're very talented and you're tops in your field," I said, looking for something she could agree was a positive right away.

"Yes," she said, her voice stronger. "I worked hard to get where I am." Then her face fell, her voice took on a bit of a whine as she continued: "But I'm tired of being sick. I'm scared."

"Your mother was an alcoholic, wasn't she?" Lexy nodded. "Are you familiar with Alcoholic Anonymous' 12 steps?" Again she nodded. "Remember the one that calls for a fearless and searching self-evaluation? You've only done half of that: You've examined all the negatives in your life. Looking at the negatives all day long, like so many people do, is one of the main reasons why people give up. It's an invitation to disaster. Let's focus on your positives instead."

I gave her a pen and continued, "I'm going to see some other patients. When I come back, I want you to have a list of your positives, starting with your career, which I know is a strong plus."

When I returned about an hour later, she presented me with the napkin on which she had jotted down her list of positives. I had thought her career would go at the top of the list, but she began with her children, and went on to mention her career, her mother, friends, some artists she had trained in the art of cartoon voices, thoughts of future grandchildren and several other positives.

"I didn't know there were so many good things in my life," she said. "Seeing this gives me courage to go on."

We worked out a program of looking only at pluses and possibilities, not the negatives. You've read enough of this book to know that many of her problems cleared up as she got rid of the negativity in her life. Some problems remained. Unfortunately, I don't have all the answers. But I can tell you that perseverance in the face of adversity is a good medicine. When you insist on persevering, you'll tell your spirit how to behave — positively!

---

The recipe for perseverance calls for generous doses of
positivity.

---

## Dare To Go On!

*Die, my dear Doctor, that's the last thing
I shall do!*

*Lord Palmerston*

These days I'm proud of Rhoda M., watching her
business and speaking career bloom. But I remember the
days not so long ago when she was recovering from a
"devastating" divorce, as she described it. She had
poured her heart into the marriage, and had also helped
her husband turn his faltering little business into a
prosperous firm. Unfortunately, he prepared well for
the divorce, hiding assets and otherwise bending the
law. She was left with almost nothing.

"What's the use?" she asked me. "I've had enough of
this garbage." Her weight and blood pressure had both
shot up as her self-esteem plummeted off the bottom of
the charts since the divorce. "I'm only here for one thing,
Dr. Fox," she told me as we sat in my office. "I want you
to put me on medicine to control my blood pressure so
I can get life insurance. Then I can die. What do you
think of that?" she asked despondently.

"Well," I answered, "you know someone cares about
you. The insurance company." She smiled a little. "It's a
start. When I get you on the medicine, your agent can sell
you a policy so he'll be happy. See? Somebody cares
about you, and you'll make at least one person happy by
staying alive. That's a plus. If you don't care about
yourself, how about that insurance agent? He's going to be

upset if you die. It's going to make him look very bad."

"That's logical, in an illogical way," she said, brightening up.

We spoke for a long time, going over and over the divorce, what her husband had done to her, and her lack of prospects for the future. Her situation was not enviable. She was broke. The rent was long past due on her apartment, and the landlord was threatening legal action. Her car was about to be repossessed. Most of her friends avoided her, fearing she'd ask them for money. She couldn't even get a reference from her last employer because he was her ex-husband whom she had worked for so long.

It was clear, however, that fear was her primary problem. She had been brutally cast aside. How was she to survive? Pay the rent? Support herself in the years ahead? Now 50 pounds heavier than usual, she feared she was no longer attractive. And she feared she had lost the ability to judge others, having made such a mistake in assessing her ex-husband's character.

I had no answers for her problems, but I knew she was a strong woman temporarily overwhelmed by adversity. I was confident she'd rally her resources and fight back, but wished there was some way I could spur her on. We talked around and around, went over diet, nutrition, positive thinking and so on. I'm afraid I didn't make much of an impression on her. She left the office as despondent as when she arrived.

The next time I saw her, however, she was a different woman. All her problems were still there, but she had taken on a new challenge. She had enrolled in a graduate business program, and was planning to become a business consultant.

"I built my ex's business up from nothing. *I* handled all the PR. *I* went out and got him new accounts. *I* hired the new people. *I* selected the location for the new plant. If I did it for him, for nothing, I can get paid to do it for others!"

Amazed at her daring, and forgetting to emphasize the positive, I asked: "How? You still don't have any money. I know you lost your apartment. How are you going to do this?"

"I don't know, but I'll do it. I dared myself to do it, and I'm going to do it. I want to prove something to myself."

Rhoda proved something to herself. She proved something to everyone else as well: *You're only as down as you think you are.* When Rhoda believed her life was ruined, it very nearly was. When she dwelled on the negative, she could think of nothing but a negative solution (suicide). But when she dared to go on, when she challenged herself to succeed, no matter what, she found a way.

Anyone can give up, that's easy. Accept the challenge: Dare yourself to go on.

---

You think winners are made? You're right. You know who makes them winners? They do, by themselves.

---

## A Secret For Being Number One

*The great are great only because we are on our knees.*

*Pierre Proudhon*

Although I was ranked number one in my class at the close of my first year in medical school, and things were looking good, by the middle of the second year I was in deep trouble. My wife had recently given birth to our first son, Howard, and we were absolutely broke. We barely had enough money to feed our baby, let alone pay rent or tuition. I had dreamed of being a doctor since the days when as a young child, I watched our kindly family doctor walking through the neighborhood to visit his patients. Through grade school, high school, the army and college, I always knew where I was headed: to medical school. Now that I was there, however, it looked as if my stay would be brief. It was one thing to ask my wife to sacrifice so that I might become a doctor, but the baby had to be fed.

At that time I was supporting my little family — that is, trying to support them — by running my own tiny pharmaceutical company out of our apartment. We kept all of our stock on a few shelves. I was the sole salesman. While she was still pregnant, my wife used to deliver the occasional small order we sold, then stand in the doctor's office looking hungry. The idea was to play on the doctor's sympathy and be paid in cash — immediately.

Our dreams of having a giant pharmaceutical company and my becoming a doctor looked as if they were about to end. I decided to withdraw from medical school at the trimester break and get a full-time job. "You'll be able to go back to school in a year or two," I told myself. But I doubted it.

As the Christmas break approached, I glumly went through the motions of going to school and visiting doctors, hoping to sell some of my wares, counting the days left until economic reality put an end to my dream of being a doctor. On the last day of the term, as I was making my rounds of doctor's offices, laboratories and hospitals, trying to make a sale, a very heavy rainstorm began. Soon the streets were almost impassable.

"This is crazy," I thought. "No other pharmaceutical representatives are out today. Not in this kind of weather. Besides, why bother? Today's my last day anyway, I'm closing up shop tomorrow. I might as well go home and forget it." But then I answered myself: "You've got to finish seeing the people on your list for today. You have a job to do, so do it." I turned my car around and headed downtown to call on the biggest clinic in town. Now, I had never even been able to get past the receptionist at this place, let alone see the head man or sell them even one bottle of medicine. But the clinic was on my list, and I was determined to do my job, no matter how bleak the possibilities.

When I walked into the usually busy clinic, I was surprised to see the doctors, nurses and receptionist sitting around, chatting. The weather was so bad, there were no patients. They were just as surprised to see me.

"What are you doing here? No other sales reps are out today!"

"I've come to see Dr. Rains, the medical director," I answered.

I had never been allowed to see Dr. Rains or anyone else before, but today I was ushered right into the head man's office. There was nothing else to do that day, so he agreed to see me. Dr. Rains was a very pleasant man. We chatted for a while, then he asked me what company I was with. When I told him I had my own company, and that I was a medical student, he said: "Kid, I like people who take chances. You've picked a perfect time. We're low in all pharmaceuticals. Get ready for a big order."

And he began reeling off the names of pharmaceuticals, ordering what for me were incredible quantities. As he ordered medicine after medicine, I mentally calculated the profit I would make: It was enough for me and my small family to survive for months! I wouldn't get the money for thirty days, and I still didn't have enough for tuition, but I didn't care! I had new hope. I knew I could make it.

Why did I get the order? Not because I was smarter or luckier than the other salesmen, or because I had better connections or a superior product. I got the order because I did my job. I went out in the rain and did my job. Sure, it helped that Dr. Rains liked people who took chances. But if any other representative had been there before me, they would have received the order.

If you do your job, opportunities will turn up to reward your perseverance.

---

Just doing your job puts you head and shoulders above the other guy.

---

There's a postscript to this story. Several months later I was called into the dean's office for nonpayment of tuition. I took my little boy, Howard, with me. Just as the dean was saying that I would either have to pay up or withdraw, he noticed that Howard was chewing on his very nice furniture. He immediately threw us out of his office. I never heard another word about my delinquent tuition.

## The Lessons of Perseverance

What lessons can we learn from these stories? First, never give in! You may be a whole lot closer to solving the problem than you think you are. Even if you're not, stay with it. This is not to say, however, that you must always charge full steam ahead. Sometimes a judicious retreat, giving you time to rest and reconsider your alternatives, is in order.

Second, it's easy to give in if you're always looking at the negative side of your life. Don't worry about the negatives; concentrate on the positive! Bolster your belief in yourself, and give your self-love a shot in the arm by emphasizing the positive aspects of your life. This will give you the courage to go on.

Third, make a challenge out of your difficulty. Tell yourself that you can do it. Now prove it by doing it. There's nothing like a good challenge to revitalize the spirit and focus your energies.

Finally, do what you're supposed to do. In many cases, we know exactly what it takes to be successful. But we're lazy or fearful or negligent. If you do your job, and do it right, you'll be way ahead of most everyone else.

## Fear: The Enemy Of Perseverance

*The only thing we have to fear is fear itself.*

### Franklin Delano Roosevelt

It sounds so easy, doesn't it? Just get out there and never give up. Unfortunately, perseverance can sometimes be very difficult. If but one weapon from your armory of virtues is missing, your sword of persistence may lose its edge.

A patient of mine, a young man named Brad, learned a lesson about perseverance when he tried to become an actor.

Moving to Los Angeles when he was only 18 years old, Brad quickly found a relatively inexpensive apartment in Hollywood, got himself a job as a waiter in an Italian restaurant and had photos taken for his resume, and found an agent. Brad instructed the agent to send him to every audition he could, as many as possible.

So Brad went to audition after audition in the next several months. Unfortunately, he was constantly turned down. He was too tall for the part, they said. He was too short for the next part, or too blond, too young-looking, too old, too WASP-ish, not WASP-ish enough. He didn't look Italian enough for this part; he didn't have enough background for that part. Too scuzzy-looking, not scuzzy enough. Once he was actually cast in a very tiny role that included a couple of lines with a famous starlet. But then the actress dropped out of the movie for some reason, and they had to get a new starlet. This new woman, however, was several inches taller than the previous one, so Brad was replaced by a taller guy.

"After two weeks of this," Brad explained, "I came to believe I was a failure. Maybe one out of ten times I was turned down because my acting wasn't good enough. The other times it was strictly because I didn't fit the director's preconceived notion of what the character is like, or I was an inch too tall, or my chin was too square.

I know that's got nothing to do with my acting, but I couldn't help but believe I was a failure. I entered into the failure mode."

Now that Brad believed he was a failure, his spirit set to work proving it. He became forgetful, irritable and anxious. He committed a multitude of small errors at work, like forgetting which table asked for the extra spaghetti sauce and adding bills up improperly. He overslept. He forgot the lines to his prepared scenes at auditions. He developed an almost-constant throbbing pain on the top of his head. His stomach was constantly upset. When he actually got a part in a low-budget theatrical play, he argued with the director so much he was fired.

"I got another role," he told me, "in a little play. Come opening night, I couldn't do it. I had so little self-confidence left, I couldn't go on. They had to cancel the show. I spent the next two months hiding in my room, telling myself what a failure I was. I never went to another audition. I was too scared. I gave up acting," he said sadly.

"Why did this happen to me?" he asked. "I persevered."

Brad had plenty of enthusiasm, plus courage to move across country and strike out on his own, but he lacked self-love (self-confidence). His self-esteem wasn't strong enough to handle the inevitable rejections every actor and artist faces. He took the turndowns personally, even though he knew they had nothing to do with his acting talent. Well, we all know that continual rejection is very painful. This young man began to believe he was a failure: not only as an actor, but as a person. His outlook on life soured with unhappy effects on his mind, body and spirit. Soon he became fearful. Too frightened to face more rejection at auditions. Too frightened to go on stage once he got the role. So frightened of everything, in fact, he dropped out entirely.

Like all actors and artists, Brad faced a great deal more rejection than the average person. But if his numbers were greater and the time span shorter, the ideas are the same. Brad lacked a plentiful supply of all the essential ingredients of perseverance and he failed. We're all rejected for one reason or another many times in life. That's why it is essential to fill ourselves with all the stuff of perseverance: belief, self-love, forgiveness and enthusiasm.

---

Fortify yourself now with the ingredients of perseverance. When difficulties come, you'll be forearmed.

---

## Ten Thousand More Tries

Fear is the chief nemesis of perseverance. How can you go out and try one more time when you're afraid? Afraid of rejection. Afraid of having another door slam in your face, of hearing yet another "no", of having another guy/girl turn you down. Afraid of failure, or maybe subconsciously afraid of success. Afraid of embarrassment or ridicule. Afraid of being shown for the loser you fear you really are.

What do you do when you must go out and try one more time, but you're afraid? Well, if fear is the enemy of perseverance, perseverance is the antidote to fear.

*Remember*, perseverance is built on the other four virtues:

enthusiasm
belief
self-love
forgiveness

When you're stuck in the mud of failure and haven't the courage to go on, give yourself a spiritual transfusion of enthusiasm, belief, self-love and forgiveness. Then you'll be able to push through the muck and continue onward. Use this affirmation for perseverance to get you started.

*I'm not giving it one more try: I'm giving it ten thousand more tries! Belief is my strong sword, enthusiasm my mighty lance. Forgiveness is my shield and self-love my impenetrable armour. Invincibly armed, I'm going to accomplish my goals!*

Repeat this affirmation over and over again, especially when you're mired in a difficult situation. Bolster your perseverance by saying the affirmations for enthusiasm, belief, self-love and forgiveness as well.

## Deep Wells Of Conviction

I once told many of these perseverance stories and others to a man who greatly doubted the value of the five virtues. He was quick to seize upon each small point as a chance to refute my arguments.

"You said perseverance requires all the virtues," he argued, "yet in each story, the person lacks at least one. How come they succeeded? Aren't you being inconsistent?" he sneered at me.

We're only human. Even the best of us can become frightened, baffled, weary and can forget our inner stength. It's happened to me more than once in my life.

I'll never forget how I wavered when called before a panel of doctors at the Los Angeles County Hospital many years ago.

Having completed a medical internship, I applied for two Residency programs (one in psychiatry at the government drug rehabilitation hospital in Lexington, Kentucky, and the other in Internal Medicine at the Los Angeles County Hospital). From Lexington came a note saying that the position was filled for the year. The Los

Angeles County Hospital wrote to say that 21 doctors had applied for their one opening in Internal Medicine. Based on a review of the applications, I was ranked last on the list. According to civil service regulations they were obligated to interview me, the note continued, but I was so far down on the list, I shouldn't waste my time going to the interview.

"Twenty-one out of twenty-one!" I thought. "That's terrible. I'll never make it." But two weeks later I was in Los Angeles, determined to persevere and beat the odds. So what if the other guys have better records? I'll charm them at the interview, I told myself.

Standing outside the medical director's office, listening to the other 20 obviously bright and well-educated candidates discussing intricacies of medicine, I began to have my doubts. They were talking knowledgeably about obscure diseases of which I knew very little. Then to make matters worse, I learned that this was not a simple interview: It was an oral test.

"I'm not prepared for a test," I told myself. "These guys must have been studying for weeks; they're going to make me look stupid."

Just then the senior Internal Medicine Resident came by and announced that he was going to take us for a tour of the hospital. I decided to go on the tour, to see what the place was like, then slip out of the door before the test. But before we took a step, the door to the medical director's office opened and my name was called. I was to be tested first. There was no way out.

Inside the office, eight very grim-looking doctors sat behind a large, highly polished mahogany desk. As I walked into the room, before I even sat down, one of them shouted at me: "What's the mechanism for a cough?" Startled, I stammered out the neural pathways along which the mechanism is initiated.

Seeing that I was flustered, the medical director said, "Sit down, Arnold. I see here on your application that you have three little children. Very nice. We're going to go around the table five times, each doctor asking you a question. That's forty questions. Are you ready?" I said I was, although I was not. Why hadn't they told me it was a test, not an interview?

The first question concerned a patient with congestive heart failure, shortness of breath and high blood pressure: How much digitalis (a heart medication) would I prescribe? I quickly answered that I may or may not use digitalis for that patient, but first I had to know more about the patient, laboratory results and so on. The doctor's face reddened as he gave me the additional information. When I gave my answer, his face got even redder. "I guess I got it wrong," I thought, my heart sinking.

The next question came immediately. A person with severe asthma is brought into the emergency room: How much adrenaline would I administer? Again I said I needed more information about the patient, such as the blood pressure reading, condition and so on. This doctor's face also reddened as he gave me the additional information, and I gave him my answer.

"They must think I'm an idiot," I thought, "asking for more information. I'll bet the others will spit out the answers immediately. I should have stayed home."

As we went around the table, doctor after doctor, I answered every single question with my own question: I needed more information. And every single time the questioner's face got very red, which I knew meant I was flunking the test. I finally left the room, certain that I had failed.

A week later I received a telegram telling me that I had been chosen for the Internal Medicine Residency at the hospital.

Many months after that, I was in the emergency room in the middle of the night with other Internists. The medical director stopped by to check on us, so I asked him why I had been chosen over the 20 other clearly well qualified candidates.

"Arn," he said, "you were the only one who requested additional information before telling us how you would treat a patient, which is what any good doctor should do. The others gave us memorized answers that took no account of the patient's clinical status."

"They all knew a lot more than I did. They knew all the obscure diseases."

"That's true, but they didn't know how to evaluate, diagnose or treat the ordinary patients that we doctors spend the overwhelming majority of our time on."

The point of this story is not that I'm so smart, because I'm not. I didn't know as much as the others. The fact that I answered the questions with questions of my own is a tribute to my teachers, who taught me that each patient is an individual with unique needs.

The point of this story is that it's okay to waver, as long as, deep within you, you have good supplies of belief, enthusiasm, self-love and forgiveness. If the wells are deep, it's all right if your faith wavers a bit. You'll persevere anyway. I had deep conviction in myself, more than I realized. But I allowed it to be shaken at the sight of my 20 very bright competitors. Luckily, my belief in myself was strong enough to withstand my temporary self-doubt. My conscious mind was worried, but my unconscious knew that I was a good doctor who knew how to treat sick patients.

Another point of this story, incidentally, is that you should always keep after your goal, no matter how smart the competition may be or how dumb you think you are. You might surprise yourself with your knowledge. Or you might happen to have that unique knowledge or background that carries the day. Never sell yourself short. Others will tell you you're no good. You tell yourself that you're great.

---

Develop deep wells of conviction. When the surface waters ripple, remember there's a calm ocean of conviction below to draw upon.

## Never Give In!

There you have the five golden virtues:
enthusiasm
belief
love
forgiveness
perseverance

**Enthusiasm** is the virtue that tells you how to act at all times: with enthusiasm, with spirit, with joy and zest for life. Enthusiasm acts on your "E-spot" to produce endorphins and other good substances that in the right balance make you feel great!

**Belief** is the virtue that instructs you how to look at yourself. Always see yourself as being worthy of the best life has to offer. No matter what your present state, exalted or low, believe in yourself wholeheartedly. When you believe you deserve the best, you set in motion events that work to bring out the best in you — and bring the best to you.

**Love** is a double virtue; self-love and love for others. Self-love, self-confidence is the basis for strong mental blueprints. Tell your spirit that you have faith in yourself. Let your spirit write that great message into your mental blueprints and make it part of the very structure of your being. Outward love, the love of others and the love of life, fills you with unlimited joy. When you live with love, you find continual delight in people and things. Love is the most powerful weapon you can wield against the fears and guilts that limit our lives and cripple our health.

**Forgiveness** is also a double virtue. Self-forgiveness greatly mitigates the guilt that is an albatross around so many of our necks. And when you forgive others, immediately and unconditionally, you free yourself from the terrible burden of carrying and nourishing hatreds and hurts forever. Having forgiven, you're free to enjoy your life.

**Perseverance** — put the first four virtues together, and you have the strength, courage and determination for the fifth: perseverance. Now turn it around: Persevere with your enthusiasm, no matter how tired or worn you may be. Persevere in your belief, no matter how great the pressure to succumb to self-doubt and feelings of failure. Persevere in your love, no matter how great the temptation to despise. Persevere in your forgiveness, regardless of the number of times you've failed yourself, or others have harmed you.

Never give in to unenthusiasma, self-doubt, guilt, anger, fear, or any of the other negatives that crush the spirit.

Never give in! Tell your spirit what to think. Insist that it always lead you forward to a better life. Never give in to anything, except unlimited joy of life.

# Goals Divided By Purpose Equals Happiness

Years ago I sat in my office talking to an accountant. "I'm not just any accountant," he boasted. "I'm the tops in my field in Beverly Hills. I have more clients than any of the others. I've got enough money to buy and sell half the accountants in this town." He went on and on about the many famous entertainers, industrialists and politicians he had as clients. Finally I held my hand up and said, "You didn't come here to tell me how rich and important you are. Let's talk about your physical and spiritual health. How are you feeling?"

He looked down at the ground, squirmed in his seat and inspected his fingernails before saying, softly; "I'm unhappy, Dr. Fox. I don't know why. Years ago I thought that if only I had X number of clients and Y number of dollars, I would be happy."

"Were you happy back then?" I asked.

"Yes. As I was getting more and more clients, I was happy. As my bank account grew, I was very happy. In a few years of hard work I achieved all my goals and more. I've got ten times the number of clients and a hundred times as much money, but I'm miserable."

"How's your family life?"

"It's a mess," he answered, again looking down. "My wife and I have been on the verge of divorce several times. I hardly ever see my kids. They don't like me. Making money doesn't give me a kick anymore. I don't care about my money anymore. Or my clients. It's got to the point where I don't want to see them. I have my assistants see them. In fact, I don't want to see anyone. I've got everything anybody can want. I have a Rolls Royce and a Jag. I don't care about any of it."

He leaned forward in his chair, dropped his voice and continued: "You're the only one I can tell this to. I was much happier when I was working my way through school as a poor bookkeeper. My wife and I loved each other. We had no money, but we had lots of dreams. Anyway, I came to see you because I'm depressed and I can't sleep." His voice dropped as he continued. "I've been having sexual difficulties lately. With my girlfriend. And last week I went into a store here in Beverly Hills to buy something I didn't need, when all of the sudden I didn't know where I was. I had no idea where I was or what I was doing. What's happening to me?"

I told him that he apparently had entered into a fugue state, an amnesia-type condition. But more important than the temporary confusion was the absence of joy and meaningful direction in his life. This man was in many ways the embodiment of the American dream. On the strength of his own intelligence and determination, he'd built an impressive accounting firm and personal fortune achieving and exceeding every single goal he had set for himself. Why then, was he so depressed? Because he lacked purpose.

---

Without a guiding purpose, life lacks meaning.

---

## Goals And Purpose

Wait a minute. This man had goals but no purpose? Aren't they the same thing? Yes, the dictionary definitions of the two words are similar, but like many I use them in a different way. Goals are things or conditions for which we strive. Goals include graduating from school, getting a job, mastering a task, finding that "special someone", earning a certain amount of money, joining a club, learning to dance or play baseball, inventing something, buying a nice house, a TV, stereo, VCR or computer, moving to a certain part of town, vacationing in Hawaii and so on.

*Goals* are great; they're like stairs we climb, going up and up as we achieve goal after goal. But where does the staircase lead? That depends on your purpose in life.

*Purpose* has to do with your spirit. Purpose is your reason for living, it's your ultimate destination in life. You may never arrive at your "destination", but without purpose, all else matters little. Purpose organizes and gives meaning to your goals. Purpose tells you *why* you want to achieve this goal or that, tells you where the staircase you're climbing leads.

Many unhappy people have many goals, but little or no purpose. They spend their lives chasing the goals, wondering all the while why they're unhappy and unhealthy. So many times the answer is simple: They lack purpose in life.

---

Goals are the steps carrying you forward. Purpose tells you where you're going — and why.

---

## Purpose To Goals Ratio

When I evaluate a patient, I look for certain balances in their body chemistry. For example, sodium is good, but too much can be harmful. Because potassium counterbalances some of the effects of sodium, I check to make sure the potassium/sodium ratio is in order. The proper potassium/sodium ratio is important in making sure we don't get high blood pressure. By the same token, your purpose and goals must be harmoniously balanced, so I ask people to figure out their Purpose To Goals (P/G) Ratio.

P = Purpose in life
G = Goals
P/G = Purpose divided by Goals

Unfortunately, I don't know how to reduce purpose and goals to numbers that can be plugged into this equation. Why then do I ask people to figure out their P/G ratio? To make them think about themselves.

How about you? Do you have a purpose in life? Have you established goals to carry you toward that purpose? Is your purpose really a purpose, or is it a goal? Many patients tell me that their purpose in life is to be rich or famous or perhaps powerful. I tell them that money, fame and power are goals, not purposes. Whether they are good or bad goals depends upon how they fit into the larger pattern of your life, which is your purpose.

Are your purpose and goals balanced? Or does one overshadow the other?

## A Low P/G Ratio

The wealthy accountant had plenty of goals but no purpose in life. I've seen many patients just like him. They're often depressed, frustrated and unhealthy. Typically, they're tired of their jobs, their associates and customers. They have poor relations with their family and friends. The things they've acquired or done mean little to them. Why? Because without purpose in life, one goal becomes as meaningless as the next.

Most of the unhappy patients I see have a low P/G ratio: plenty of goals, but no purpose. Desperately looking for something — anything — to make themselves happy, they often turn to money. Amassing huge sums of money and buying lots of expensive things becomes the driving force in their lives. They think the quest for cash is their purpose in life, but it's not. It's only a shot in the dark, one which has no chance of hitting the ultimate target in life: happiness.

People with low P/G ratios may suffer from a wide variety of emotional and physical ills, such as depression, fatigue, listlessness, irritability, poor personal relationships, sexual difficulties, aches and pains, sleep disturbances, gastrointestinal upsets of various kinds and on and on. The list is frightening and very long.

The accountant I described was experiencing some of these problems. Unfortunately, his situation progressed to become terminal.

## Goal-aholics

After listening to the unhappy accountant's story, I carefully took his medical and personal history, performed a thorough physical examination and called for the appropriate tests. He was suffering from a variety of illnesses related to his depression. His immune system, battered by the high-voltage chemicals associated with depression, had been knocked for a loop. After beginning him on a treatment program, I told the man that he must find a purpose in life if he wanted to be healthy and happy.

"I had a purpose in life years ago," he told me. "Back in college I wanted to use the tax system to help the little people. That's why I became an accountant. Perhaps I could go back to that purpose."

I agreed that was a good idea. "When you lost your purpose," I explained, "you turned to goals. You became a goal-aholic concentrating on two goals: making money and getting more clients. Like an alcoholic, the goal-aholic is headed toward self-destruction, toward broken health and/or death. It's time to return to your purpose in life. Your goals will fall into place. You'll have that old enthusiasm back. Many of your physical problems will take care of themselves."

He seemed excited at the prospect of rediscovering his purpose in life. He left in high spirits. Although I never saw him again, I learned through mutual friends that the next two years were a time of renewed energy, health, joy and interest in life for this man. He stopped counting his case files. He only took cases that interested him or were for a good cause, and began giving free lectures on the tax system. He spent more time with his family.

Unfortunately, goal-aholics, like alcoholics, face a lifelong struggle. This unfortunate goal-aholic couldn't resist falling into old habits, looking to numbers and goals for happiness. Eventually he left his wife and went through a succession of pretty young girlfriends. He paid no attention to his children, preferring to lavish his attention on girls and cars, on travel to Paris, Monte Carlo and Las Vegas. None of it made him happy, however. Not the girls, not the high living, not the cars. More and more important names were added to his client list, greater and greater sums to his fortune. One day I picked up the paper to find his obituary. I later discovered that he had committed suicide, the ultimate goal-aholic act.

---

The goal-aholic grabs for goals like a dying man gasping for breath. But in the absence of purpose, goals have little meaning.

---

## A High P/G Ratio

What of the reverse situation, a very high P/G ratio: lots of purpose but few goals? Is that good or bad?

A high P/G ratio means that you have a purpose in life, but few plans for fulfilling that purpose. That can be very frustrating.

Let me tell you about a young man with a high P/G ratio.

Phil came to my office complaining of stomach pains, diarrhea, bloody stool, headaches and "jitters". After taking a complete personal and medical history and performing a thorough physical examination, including a gastroscopy (a look into his stomach using a flexible tube passed through the mouth), I sat down in my office with him to review my findings.

"You have a bleeding ulcer," I told him. "That accounts for the stomach pain, diarrhea and bloody stool. I found no organic reason for your headaches and jitters. They may be a reaction to the ulcer, but I think there's something else troubling you."

"Sure, Dr. Fox, I'll tell you what's wrong. Everytime I go outside and see the smog I get upset. We're destroying our environment. We're wiping out animal species every day, we're poisoning our own food and water and air. We're turning the planet into a big garbage dump that our kids are going to have to live in . . . if they can. I wish I could do something about it."

"So what are you doing about it?" I asked.

"Nothing," he answered, surprised. "What can any-body do about it? I'd love to do something. I think about it all the time, but what?"

"I can give you medicine for your ulcer and headaches, and tranquilizers for your jitters, but I know you're too smart to get caught up in drugs and their side effects. Instead, how about some advice from an older man? Much of your illness comes from the fact that you're eating yourself up inside. You've got a great purpose, cleaning up the environment, but you're not doing anything about it. Except making yourself sick."

"What could I possibly do?"

"You could write books. You could become a Ralph Nader-type lobbyist. You could organize boycotts and protests. You can try to get celebrities to give benefits. You can become a professor and teach a generation of students about ecology. You could start an educational foundation. There are plenty of things you can do."

A bright fellow, Phil quickly understood why he was ill, and that he could set up goals to carry him toward his purpose. About a year later he came in for a checkup. Needless to say, his ulcer and other problems were long forgotten. "I'm head of my own non-profit ecology group," he proudly informed me. "I still don't know how much of a difference my little group will make realistically speaking," he said, "but it feels great to be heading somewhere to have a purpose!"

---

Purpose without goals leads to a chasm forming between your desires and your perceived abilities. Frustration and anger build up as you come to see yourself as a failure.

---

## The Perfect P/G Ratio

The ideal P/G ratio represents a flexible balance between your goals and your purpose in life. Imagine that you can see your purpose at the end of a long road. All along that road are your goals, one after another, landmarks telling you that you're headed in the right direction, that you're making good progress. With a balanced P/G ratio, you'll find yourself traveling down that road at a satisfying rate, moving from goal to goal at just the right speed.

If I had to choose a number, I would say that the perfect P/G ratio is one. With a P/G ratio of one, your goals and purpose are in perfect harmony. The great Dr. Albert Schweitzer, for example, had a wonderful and noble purpose in life: to help the poor and oppressed. His goals were to set up a hospital in Africa, and assist people who came to him for treatment. Those goals were perfectly suited to his purpose, giving him a P/G ratio of one. Mother Teresa is another saintly example of a person with a tremendous purpose in life and an ideal P/G ratio. She is such a selfless person, in fact, that her purpose in life is almost identical with her goals.

You don't have to be like Dr. Schweitzer or Mother Teresa to have a good P/G ratio. All you have to do is find a good purpose in life, one that you enjoy aspiring to; then set up a series of goals to guide you to that purpose. I know of one woman whose noble purpose in life is to alleviate hunger. Two full days a week she works on the soup lines, helping to feed the hungry and homeless people of Los Angeles. She has established a goal (assisting on the soup line) that carries her toward her purpose in life.

## Choosing Purpose

"Okay, Dr. Fox," some patients say. "Tell me what my purpose should be."

I can't answer that on a one-to-one basis, although I have helped people find their own purpose. My purpose in life is to teach people that they have the power to make themselves healthy and happy. To love and to be loved is an excellent purpose in life. So is being the best person you possibly can; adding joy and happiness to the world; helping reduce hunger or poverty and helping other people. There are many satisfying and worthwhile purposes to pursue.

The best purposes are other-directed: that is, they're designed to help others. It's all right if pursuing your purpose brings you wealth, power or fame. That's great, in fact, as long as your purpose is based on helping others. The "others" can be as large a group as the hungry people of the world. Or the "others" may be a very small group, such as your family. You can often discover your purpose in life in your dreams. What is it you really want to do? Not what you have to do to make a living, or what you've fallen into. What do you dream of?

## Success Is In The Journey, Not The Destination

Don't worry about whether or not you can achieve your purpose, whether you can accomplish all your goals. Goals are the stepping stones and purpose in your ultimate destination, but you don't necessarily have to "get there" to be both happy and successful. Some purposes, such as eliminating hunger or cleaning up the environment, are large and difficult tasks that may not be achieved in our lifetime. Simply striving toward your own good purpose, whatever it may be, makes you a success. Happiness is more in the journey and the struggle than it is in the accomplishment.

---

Happiness in life comes from the journey toward the ultimate goal: your purpose in life.

---

# Changing Purpose

Before we go any further, let me assure you that you're not locked into a single purpose in life. If the need arises, you can find a new purpose. Oftentimes a change of purpose, a new direction, will help you break out of an unhappy rut.

As a child, student and young doctor, I had a strong purpose in life: to help people by being a good doctor. So I mastered the knowledge and techniques taught in medical school. To keep up with advances in medicine, I read numerous medical journals and books, and attended as many conferences and lectures as possible. I must admit that I was almost arrogantly proud of my knowledge and skills. But I had my purpose firmly fixed in mind. It gave me the determination and energy to go on.

Soon, however, I found myself preoccupied with numbers, like the unhappy accountant. How many gastroscopies (using a flexible tube to look into a person's stomach) had I performed this morning? How many electrocardiograms had I read? How many reports had I dictated? How many histories had I taken?

If that were not bad enough, I came to realize through the years that I was not accomplishing my purpose in life. You see, much of what we doctors were doing in the name of medicine was not helping our patients. In fact, we were often harming the very people who came to us, so full of trust, asking for help.

"Why am I doing this?" I wondered. "Why am I looking into people's stomachs, diagnosing a bleeding ulcer, giving them medicine and sending them on their way? Why am I doing that when I know the real problem is alcoholism? It's the lack of purpose in life that calls for alcohol to dull the unhappiness that burns holes in so many stomachs, not some mysterious disease. Sure, the medicine will make their stomach feel a little better, but it won't cure the real problem. Why am I telling these people that the medicine will take care of them, when I know they'll be back in my office soon with another ulcer, or some other problem related to their drinking?"

Still, I enjoyed being a doctor. I was helping many people. There was excitement, life-and-death drama, power, ego-gratification. And I was proud to be sharing a practice with two excellent young cardiologists. But I wasn't satisfied that I was doing all that I could to help people. There was doubt groping about for a new path. One day I enrolled in law school. It was a lark, a challenge and perhaps a searching for other ways to help people.

Dissatisfaction which was bubbling under the surface erupted with volcanic force and devastation when my mother contracted leukemia (a type of cancer). Watching her slowly waste away, painfully enduring the agonies of chemotherapy before finally dying, forced me to admit that I could not achieve my purpose in life: I could not really help people by being a "good doctor". Not if being a "good doctor" meant using harsh chemicals in an attempt to cure diseases that could have been prevented. Not if being a "good doctor" meant prescribing drugs and performing procedures I knew to be dangerous to the patient. Not if being a "good doctor" meant watching helplessly as people became diseased and depressed, unable to live life to its fullest. If that's what a "good doctor" does, I decided, I don't want to be a "good doctor".

Right then and there I was a candidate for depression and/or illness. I was liable to find myself, like the accountant, without a purpose. Luckily, I quickly found a new purpose in life: helping people live long, healthy and happy lives by preventing disease from striking in the first place. With this new purpose firmly in mind, old dissatisfactions and disappointments vanished while a myriad of new goals sprang to mind. It seemed as if I were, in a sense, reborn. Looking back, I can see that I've achieved some of my goals. Others have been more difficult. Still others — some anticipated, others unexpected — have sprung up from time to time.

The point of this story is that your purpose can change. If need be, you can find a new purpose, modify the old one, or add secondary purposes.

---

Your purpose gives direction and meaning to your life.
Nothing says you can't change course if the need arises.

---

## Goals Are Not Monuments

Your goals are not written in stone either. Goals can and should change throughout your life. Otherwise, well, let me tell you about a 34-year-old woman named Kathy, who came to see me the other day.

Kathy is an urban planner whom I met while giving a talk on the relationship between thoughts and the immune system to a Los Angeles executive women's group.

A few weeks after the talk Kathy came to see me at my office. "While you were discussing the immune system and what can go wrong with it," she said, "I realized that there must be something wrong with mine. Otherwise, why would I come down with so many colds and runny noses?"

Like many patients, Kathy brought along a bag full of medicines. "These are the latest antibiotics prescribed. These," she said, pointing to another bottle, "are antibiotics given to me two months ago, and these are from six months ago," she said.

"And these are the antihistamines," I said, pointing to a bottle, "and these are the vasoconstrictors, and these are the analgesics. You've got a nice little pharmacy."

"Well," she smiled. "Check out my immune system."

I examined her carefully and took a thorough history but found nothing wrong with her, so I used various special blood tests to evaluate her immune system. The following week she returned to my office. I gave her a copy of my findings and the lab tests, and proceeded to discuss the information with her.

I told her that her immune system was indeed askew. The total T-cell count was low, and the T4/T8 ratio, an important indicator of immune system function, was off-balance.

She was aghast. "How can my immune system be so weak? I've been following your writings for years. I eat your Beverly Hills Medical Diet, and I exercise four days a week. You checked my supplement program last week and said it was good. What am I doing wrong?"

"Well," I said, "you told me you have a good relationship with your husband. How about work. What's that like?"

"It's exciting," she answered. "I got into the company through the administrative side. It was a good job, but you always had to fight for change. And I saw that the real excitement was in the actual urban planning, so I went to school at night for five years. It was a real fight to get through, but I got my degree. But it's not all smiles," she said with a frown. "I'm a woman competing against men who have 20, 30 years experience in the field. I have to work extra hard and fight to prove myself."

"They make you work harder?" I asked.

"Over Labor Day weekend I took home enough work for six days. The closest I got to having fun was looking out my window at the marina. I wanted to be out there sailing, but I have to show them I'm better than they are."

"They said that?"

"No, they don't say anything. But I *know* I have to prove to them I'm capable, even if I am a woman."

We spoke more about her job, then I suggested, "Kathy, it's time you stopped fighting the old battle. You had certain goals: to get a job with the company, go to school, get a degree, become an urban planner. You had to fight to achieve those goals. You had to prove yourself to your bosses, to your teachers and most of all to yourself. Now you think you have to fight with your co-workers to prove yourself. You don't. You've told me they have been helpful, and that they treat you with professional respect. You've made it, you've fought all the battles and you've won. Now stop fighting. You're like an immune system with too many helper cells prodding it on to fight enemies that don't exist. You're the only loser in the battle. There are no winners. Back off before you send yourself to the hospital. Don't let old, useless goals get in your way."

---

The road of life has many unexpected twists, turns and detours. Keep your goals — your road map — flexible and up-to-date or you may find yourself upside down in a ditch.

---

## Rediscovering Purpose In Life

The accountant I described earlier had a purpose when he was young, using his knowledge of tax accounting to help others. Unfortunately, he lost that purpose, and was unable to return to it successfully. Others, however, have been able to rediscover their purpose in life before it was too late. Let me tell you about one man who did just that.

A few months ago a doctor called me and said that he had some new high-tech equipment for imaging the body, the latest hardware for looking in the brain, heart, lungs and other parts.

"Frankly," he said, "I'd like you to send me patients. Would you come over and see my equipment, then have lunch with me?" I agreed, and on the appointed day went to his office in West Los Angeles.

This was the first time I had met Dr. Tom, a handsome 40-year-old doctor. Looking very businesslike in a three-piece suit, he showed me around his large and very well equipped office. In one room a patient was having her brain checked out by a CT scanner. Two technicians monitored images of her brain on video screens as the machines hummed softly in the background. It was very impressive. We went through all the rooms, gazing at the futuristic-looking equipment as Dr. Tom rattled off an impressive stream of medical jargon — medial this, posterior that, magnetic resonance and what have you — pointing to screens and pushing buttons as computers went through their paces and lights flashed on and off. Finally we went to a fancy restaurant in Century City.

"Would you like some wine?" he asked as we sat down. When I declined, he smiled and said: "I'm glad. Some of the doctors I've taken to lunch drank so much they didn't hear a word I said."

Dr. Tom spoke about his equipment for a while. Then he stopped, smiled softly, "You weren't very impressed, were you?"

"No," I answered. "You've got a lot of interesting machinery, but I could see that you were showing me around in a very perfunctory manner. Even now you're only half-heartedly giving me the sales pitch."

"It's that noticeable?" he asked ruefully.

"You're obviously bored with your machines. You know what? You told me all about the machines, how many reports you can generate a day, how much of the body you can scan, how the machines will help doctors, how many this and that, but you never once said anything about the patients, how your equipment will help the patients. From what I saw of the office, it seems that your technicians do all the work. Your private office is far away from the patients, and you have a private entrance in back. You've arranged everything so you never have to see a patient. Why did you become a doctor? I know it's not because you love those machines."

"You know, Arnold," he said. "I had a reason for being a doctor when I was young. You see, my family was sick a lot, especially my mother. As a little boy I decided to become a doctor and find cures for my family. But in medical school I started to become afraid of patients. I didn't want to have to deal with them. I guess I was afraid I couldn't help them."

He learned forward in his chair and continued. "I never thought about this, Arn. But I should. I think I began to feel inadequate in my ability to deal directly with patients, so I decided to go into radiology, where I don't have to see them much. Now I've got this high-tech imaging center, but no reason for being a doctor. Or anything else, for that matter. You're right. I'm bored. I didn't want to look at a patient. I haven't even thought about curing people's problems, which is why I became a doctor in the first place. That's what's been tearing me apart."

By now I was starving but he was too excited to eat. He kept waving the tuxedoed waiter away. So we continued talking, and I told him about goals and purpose, comparing them to something he was familiar with:

computer hardware and programs. Goals are like computer hardware (the screen, the disc drives, the keyboard and all the other things you can touch). They're great. But without the right programming (purpose) telling the hardware what to do, the computer is worthless.

"Yes!" he said excitedly. "This is so right on! I've got a program in me that says, 'Watch out, stay away from 'patients.' So I expanded that and I'm staying away from everybody — my family, my friends, even my employees. I've been hiding in my office and thinking about money. How many CT scans do I have to do a month to pay the rent? How many magnetic resonance images will pay the equipment loans and so on? I only took you to lunch so I could get more business!" His face fell and his voice dropped as he asked: "Am I a jerk or what?"

"Not at all," I reassured him. "You're just a man without purpose. You had a purpose once. Find it again, and you'll be all right."

---

Forgotten or discarded purposes are easily reclaimed.

---

## Goals Or Numbers?

For over 30 years I've had the opportunity to listen to doctors as they talked in doctors' dining rooms, lounges and dressing rooms, in surgical suites, at hospital meetings, in classrooms, and at social gatherings. What is one of the big topics of conversation? Numbers. Plastic surgeons talk about the number of face lifts, tummy tucks or nose jobs they've done that month. Proctologists talk about how many hemorrhoids they cut out or zapped with lasers. My cardiology friends talk about the number of pacemakers they've implanted, how many cardiac catherizations they did this week, how many times they were able to dissolve a blood clot or use a balloon catheter to flatten out an obstruction in a coronary artery.

Physicians aren't the only professionals who are number oriented, of course. CPAs think in terms of the number of clients they have, as do lawyers and most other professionals. Students count the number of pages they're required to read, and the number of questions on a test. No, doctors aren't the only guilty parties. I only single them out because I'm one of them.

For doctors, the number game begins in training. Surgical residents are required to operate on so many gall bladders, stomachs, hemorrhoids, appendixes, etc., in order to advance. Notice I said they must perform so many operations, not that they must work with people who need help. Medical students learn that you don't work on people with gall bladder problems; you operate on gall bladders.

Your teachers and the medical boards don't want to know about the people you've helped. They're interested in the numbers. How many organs did you take out? How many bones did you set? How many arteries did you scrape clean? How many X-ray and electrocardiograms did you read? How many vertebral discs or uteruses did you remove?

Early on in training, humanity is pushed aside by the numbers. Early on the idea of purpose, which is hardly ever mentioned in medical school anyway, is bred out of the fledgling doctor by the mad rush for numbers. And, oh yes, the procedures.

The young doctor in training learns that if he or she can learn to push an instrument down through the patient's mouth into the stomach and intestine, or up from the rectum into the cecum (the beginning of the large intestine), or perhaps manipulate a needle into the liver or push a plastic catheter up through an artery in the right groin into the heart, they'll be rewarded. What's the reward? More numbers: a good starting salary, a fat bank account, a big house, an expensive car, a large portfolio of stocks or ownership of apartment houses. Is it any wonder so many dedicated young men and women have lost their purpose by the time they become doctors? Is it any wonder that so many of my doctor friends are unhappily casting about for something to give meaning to their lives?

Although the story I'm going to tell you now seems outrageous, it's true.

A certain attending physician taught medical students many years ago, right here in Los Angeles. Some of the students thought this doctor — whom I'll call Dr. Slicemup — was great because he had mastered the numbers. He operated on more patients every day than most doctors did in a week. Big fees and rapid turnover earned him a fancy house right on the golf course and a flashy sports car everyone envied (you know the one: it costs as much as a house, goes from 0 to 60 in half a second and makes so much noise that everyone turns to look at you).

He must be good, his students thought, because he performs surgery for the stars, goes to Hollywood parties and flies to New York to treat Mr. Richbucks. And, oh yes, he even has a membership to the Friars Club in Beverly Hills where all the actors hang out.

These students admire Dr. Slicemup, but they also joke about him: "Be careful when you go to sleep in the doctors lounge — Dr. Slicemup will get you. That guy will operate on anybody. You lie down on a table and he'll cut you open."

What they don't know is that he plays cards and drinks at the Friar's Club until the early morning because he hates to go home to his wife and children. His wife can't stand him, neither can his kids. They only talk to him when they need money. His students notice that his hands shake constantly. That's why he has the younger doctors assisting him sew up all the incisions. He wants the scars to look nice. It's great that he wants to make sure the patients have a nice invisible scar on the outside. But what are his shaky hands doing to the insides of his patients?

Yes, many doctors-in-training admire him. If only they knew how little he thought of himself. But he can't tell them not to do what he did because he's never been honest with anyone, not even himself. He can't tell them not to do what he's done, because that would be a loss of face, another blow to his tottering self-image. He and I have talked. He wants desperately to get some meaning and purpose into his life. He'd like to know that he's done more than rack up thousands and thousands of unnecessary and often poor surgeries. He's afraid to look back at the trail of walking wounded he's left behind — and those he sent to early graves.

So many numbers. Dr. Slicemup was a role model for the young doctors. What did he teach them, aside from the art of making lots of money?

---

Don't pin all your hopes on numbers and goals. For goals are like freeway signs: You can see them from a long way off, you can feel yourself rushing forward but then suddenly the signs are gone, and you're moving away from them as fast as you once moved toward them. Who was the richest man in Jerusalem? No one knows. No one cares. But we all remember the monumental teachings of one very poor man.

---

## Burnout!

A few years ago I staged a "South Philadelphia in Los Angeles" party and reunion for all of us in Southern California who grew up in South Philly. It was great fun, what with the music and dances of yesteryear, the foods we ate as children and even some surprise reunions of old friends. I ran into Bob, an old friend I hadn't seen in over 30 years. What a disappointment! Gone was the energy, enthusiasm, good cheer and never-ending supply of jokes I remembered from our youth. Instead I saw a disillusioned, depressed and bitter man.

"Life lost its kick, Arnie," he explained, "even though I've done well for myself. Remember I used to talk about taking over my father's butcher shop, expanding it, opening a chain of butcher shops, starting a little academy to train butchers the right way?"

"Yes," I nodded.

"I did everything I said I would," he replied. "And you know what? I don't give a damn! The thing is, Arnie, I never wanted to be a butcher in the first place. If I don't ever see another piece of meat, that'll be fine by me. I see you're looking at me like 'what happened to him?' I'll tell you what happened. I'm all burned out."

Achieving goals can make you happy — very happy. *But only if the goals are part of a larger purpose and if they are your own goals.*

Bob took over his father's butcher shop only because his family pressured him into it. Yes, he achieved the goals he'd set out for himself, but they were not *his* goals, and they were not related to *his* purpose in life. What Bob really wanted to do was communicate with people through his painting. That desire, however, was frustrated by the great amount of time he spent every day, year after year, building the butcher shop chain. And so Bob became a victim of burnout: lots of goals and lots of success, all entirely unrelated to his purpose, which was never pursued. And lots of unhappiness.

Like the accountant, Bob was in trouble. Fortunately, my old friend decided it was time to make a change. He sold the butcher business and at the age of 55 took up painting. I spoke with him a little while ago.

"Never been happier, Arn," he said. "It's like it was when I was a kid. I've got something to look forward to again."

## Burnout Checklist

Burnout has to do with the stress of expectations — expectations that are never realized. Typically, burnout victims are hard-driving people who place all of their faith in goals — but not their own goals, goals imposed upon them by others. If they fail to achieve the goals, they're unhappy. If they make the goals, well, they're still unhappy because they didn't have the opportunity to fulfill their purpose in life.

Are you a victim of burnout? Check off the signs of burnout that apply to you:

(     ) Difficulty in relaxing
(     ) Increasing cynicism
(     ) Disenchantment
(     ) Feeling great pressure to succeed
(     ) Increasing boredom
(     ) Feeling a need to generate excitement over and over again
(     ) Having little time for vacation and fun with your family
(     ) Automatically expressing negative feelings
(     ) Increasing irritability and a "short fuse"
(     ) Disappointment with yourself and others
(     ) Having little time for recreation and no hobbies
(     ) A lack of intimacy with family, lover, friends
(     ) Inability to say "no" to more work, even though you're already overworked
(     ) A feeling that life is no fun
(     ) An inability to laugh at yourself
(     ) Rarely speaking at gatherings, and then only speaking negatively
(     ) Feeling that sex is more trouble than it's worth
(     ) Difficulty in setting goals
(     ) Feeling that people "use" you
(     ) Finding yourself further and further behind at the end of each day
(     ) Forgetting deadlines, appointments, etc.

If you've checked more than two or three of the items, you may be becoming a victim of burnout.

The purpose that guides your life must be your own, and your goals must lead you to that purpose. Otherwise you are at great risk of burnout.

## A Young Man With Purpose

Before closing the book on goals and purpose, read this case history. It has a happy beginning, middle and end. I'm very pleased to be able to tell you this story. You'll know why when you read it.

I have a lot of children, and I'm proud of each of them in a different way. My eldest son is named Howard. He's 33 years old now, which is interesting because my wife tells everyone she's 27. Howard married while he was in college and worked his way through law school, employed as a law clerk. He and his wife did it on their own. By the time he took and passed the California State Bar exam, he had two children.

When he went for his very first job interview, Howard did something which made me very proud and convinced me that he would never have a problem with purpose because he knew exactly what he wanted. What he did was risky, for he had a wife and family to support. This is what he told the lawyer, his prospective boss, during the interview: "I want you to understand, before you hire me, that my wife and my family come first. I will do my work, and do it very well, but unless there's an emergency, I'm not taking my work home with me. I will do more work in 40 hours than anyone else does in 60, but I must have time to spend with my wife and family."

The chief lawyer gulped and swallowed hard. So did I, when Howard told me this. After all, there's an oversupply of lawyers here in Los Angeles. Plenty of young lawyers are willing to work 60 or 80 hours a week. But

Howard had a purpose in life: giving his family the best he had to offer, including himself at home, sharing life with them.

The first firm that interviewed Howard hired him. I know the head lawyer could not help but be impressed by Howard's honesty and his devotion to his family. I'm sure he realized that a person with these two qualities is a gem.

## I See Purpose

I put this discussion of goals and purpose right after the five virtues because goals and purpose complement the virtues. Belief tells you that you're headed straight ahead, of course, but you need goals and purpose to help you direct your energies and recognize the landmarks on the way. Purpose gives you an outward-focused direction. Purpose allows you to channel your energies into worthwhile projects.

Here are the purpose and goal affirmations I want you to say everyday, as many times as possible. Repeating them over and over again will help fix your mind on your purpose in life, and help you achieve your goals, one after another.

---

*I am joyfully accomplishing my purpose in life, realizing that purpose gives me the direction and meaning I need to lead a happy and successful life. With purpose firmly in mind, I see myself rapidly accomplishing goal after goal, always moving closer and closer to my wonderful and worthwhile purpose in life.*

*I see purpose everywhere because I see it in myself.*

---

As you repeat these purpose and goal affirmations many times during the day, use your mind's eye to see yourself achieving goal after goal as you strive toward your purpose.

You deserve to have the best possible purpose in life. What is the best possible purpose? The one that makes you happy, healthy and in love with life.

# Dig In At The Banquet Of Life

*Life's a banquet but most poor bastards are starving.*

*Dolly Levy*

In Proverbs it says: "Where there is no vision, the people perish." That's true, and it's even more specifically true that where there is no vision of joy, the spirit withers and dies.

Our world is neither all good nor all bad. Life is a mixture, a tossed salad of goods, bads, greats, terribles and indifferents. Fortunately, most of life's ingredients are goods or greats, although those bads seem so large when they occur. As you examine your life, your combination of goods and bads, acknowledge the negatives, decide how to deal with them, then push them aside. Your job is to concentrate on life's joys, for it's from joy that you draw your spiritual nourishment. Always keep the vision of joy in the forefront of your mind. Dig in to your joy with gusto.

171

## When Vision Is Lacking

*What a wonderful life I've had! I only wish
I'd realized it sooner.*

*Colette*

Let me tell you about a man who had no vision of joy.
All he could see were the negatives. He was addicted to
negativism. An extremely wealthy industrialist, he came
to see me because his wife told him to. He hadn't felt well
for years, although he had not been terribly ill either. Like
many other unhappy people, he existed in that grey area
between health and disease. His wife brought him to me,
hoping I could find a disease or something to explain why
he was so negative all the time. After taking a complete
personal and medical history, performing a physical
examination and the appropriate tests, I met with the
man and his wife in my office to discuss my findings.
When I announced that I had found no organic problem
responsible for his run-down feelings, she offered her
own opinion:

"His negative attitude toward everything is the
problem," she said. "If you say it's a good day; he says it's
bad. If you say his car is nice; he says it doesn't run well.
If you say our daughters are good; he says they're bad."

"Tell me about your daughters," I asked the man.

"Which one?"

"Either."

"The fat one or the crazy one?" he asked with a chuckle.

"Do you hear what you're calling your daughters? Is
that how you really feel about them?"

"Well, no, you know, I like them. I'm proud of them.
They've both done well on their own."

"Why do you refer to them as being fat and crazy?"

"Oh, I don't really mean it. That's just what I call
them."

"Do they know that?" He nodded. "How do they like
it?"

"Hey, don't make such a big deal out of it!" he answered defensively. "It's just what I call them."

Now his wife spoke again. "They hate it. He's so negative, he drove them away. He drives everyone away."

We talked on and on, until finally he let down his guard and asked: "Do you think I like pushing people away? Do you think I like being unhappy all the time?"

"No," I replied. "It's a habit with you. You automatically react negatively, regardless of how you really feel because you have little vision of joy in your life."

"I don't know any other way to be," he admitted plaintively. "How can I break out of this?"

"By always looking for the joy in life," I answered.

"What joy?" he asked dismally.

"Your two daughters have done well on their own. You have a wife who loves you enough to stick with you. You're rich so you don't have to worry about paying the rent and buying food like a lot of people do. There's three pieces of joy right there."

"Eh!" he grunted unimpressed.

"Do you really mean that?" I asked. "Or is that your habitual response to the world?" He didn't answer.

Like so many of us, this man was addicted to negativism. To be addicted means to be devoted to a practice or habit, to be habituated, accustomed, disposed or inclined to. Addictions are a frightening part of modern life. Millions are addicted to alcohol, our most popular drug. It's a cheap and easy way to dull the pain that fills so many lives. Smoking is a terrible addiction that claims over 400,000 lives a year in this country alone. There are addictions to illegal drugs, such as cocaine, something I see a lot of among my Beverly Hills patients. And don't forget the legal drugs so many are hooked on: Valium, Demerol, Talwin and others.

As if substance addictions were not bad enough, millions of us are addicted to failure. Our self-love is so small we can't see ourselves successful. The thought that we might accomplish something — anything — simply does not compute. There are those addicted to overeating, or to eating certain kinds of foods they know are not good for them. An awful lot of us fall into this category. Some go the other way, starving and/or vomiting themselves to near death.

You probably know someone who's addicted to dangerous behaviors. One of my patients, a beautiful teenage girl, was into the punk rock scene. Her nights were a mind-numbing series of music, alcohol and drugs. Her mother and father with their old-fashioned virtues couldn't understand her. Whenever they tried to straighten her out, she would scream "I hate you" and run out of the house. Finally she wound up in the hospital, having an overdose of drugs pumped out of her stomach. When I spoke with her later, she admitted she had been terrified by her behavior for a long time. She was afraid she would wind up dead, but didn't know how to stop.

Can you be addicted to being in love? Sure. One of my patients is a 37-year-old woman who cannot seem to function unless she is "madly in love" with a man. The problem is that after three or four months with a new fellow, the glow fades. Then she's frantic and depressed, looking wildly around for someone to be "madly in love" with once again.

We're addicted because we get a psychologic, physio-logic and/or a social "lift" from our behavior. Giving in to our addictions makes us feel good. And even though we know that the "high" is temporary and our actions ultimately destructive, we give in to our addictions again and again.

The wealthy industrialist was strongly addicted to his negativism. He seemed to derive a perverse pleasure from being joyless, as well as from taking joy from others. But as he finally admitted, being unhappy all the time is no fun at all.

### You're Never Angry For The Reason You Think You Are

*. . . let not the sun go down on your wrath.*

*Ephesians 4:26*

A special note on anger, that destructive negation of the five virtues. Anger is a germ, a plague that destroys mind and body. Anger is a kind of madness that blinds our eye, boils the blood and invariably shortens our life. Anger has its own spot in the brain, like the "E-spot", where it triggers the excessive release of high-voltage substances that rampage through the body, destroying health and happiness like a fire consuming a house made of straw.

There are many negations of the five virtues. We've touched upon some of them, such as guilt and disbelief. Anger is perhaps the worst, not only because it is so violently destructive of our health and happiness but because it is so prevalent. And because so many people are addicted to their anger.

Some people tell me they feel strong when they're angry. I say we're wrong when we're angry. Not only are we harming ourselves by negating the five virtues, 99 times out of 100, we don't even know why we're angry. We have no clue.

What is anger? Anger is the dumping-ground of negative thoughts, the catch-all emotion we use to express a variety of unhappy impulses. First and foremost, anger is fear and insecurity: I'm going to lose my job. I'm going to lose status. I'm going to lose face. I'm going to lose a loved one. I'm going to lose money. I feel threatened so I respond with anger.

Anger is guilt: Instead of acknowledging the problem, omission or wrong-doing that prompts our guilt, we turn on the person we think "made" us feel guilty. It becomes their fault. "Why don't you get off my back?!" we snarl. Or, "Hey, it's not my fault!" Perhaps we counterattack saying: "Yeah? Who are you to point the finger?"

Fear and guilt: Remember how they bear down on love?

Anger is hostility and indignation: That son-of-a-bitch gave me a rough time. People are always pushy and rude. I don't get the respect I deserve. My neighbor runs his power lawnmower at seven o'clock on Saturday morning and there's nothing I can do about it.

People are often completely unaware of the fact that they're filled to the brim with free-floating, unresolved hostility. Anger is a convenient release for that hostility, even though the target of your ire has nothing to do with what's really bothering you.

Anger is frustration and resentment: People don't listen to me. He got the promotion that should have been mine. I could have been captain of the team, but the coach didn't like me. Life keeps playing nasty tricks on me. I can't make my spouse understand that things should be done my way. I feel frustrated, so I respond with anger.

Anger is all these feelings and more. Now, if we had less fear and insecurity within us, less guilt, less hostility and indignation, less frustration and resentment, we'd have less cause to become angry.

Anger also is often a habit, an addiction. We get mad because . . . well, just because . . . that's why.

Most of the time, anger is anything but what it seems. Everytime, however, anger is a negation of joy.

## Vision Of Joy

*For he that will love life and see good days . . . let him eschew evil and do good; let him seek peace and ensue it.*

*I Peter 3:10-11*

Is it possible to break bad addictions, addictions of the body and mind? Yes. You may require medical and/or psychological assistance, especially for substance abuse. The road to recovery is not always smooth and short, but the road exists. And I have found that the more enthusiasm, belief, love, forgiveness and perseverance you have, the greater the odds you'll develop a vision of joy.

Why do we become addicted? The reasons are many and complex. Generally, the problem involves lack of the five virtues. If you don't like yourself, destructive behavior doesn't seem so terrible. If you're full of unresolved anger, hurting others may feel good. When you lack self-love, it's easy to do what the others do just so they'll accept you. Those who believe little in themselves may find it easy to become addicted to failure.

Use the five virtues to develop a vision of joy. Become addicted to joy, to enthusiasm, to belief, to love, forgiveness and perseverance. Let unlimited enthusiasm raise your endorphins and make you feel great! Strengthen your self-esteem, and dangerous compulsions will drop away. Increase your forgiveness of yourself and of others, and you'll throw away much of the anger and guilt that leads you to act so destructively.

None of us are immune to temptation. Anyone can fall into bad habits. So develop inexhaustible supplies of the five virtues. Let them be your shield against harm.

## Think On These Things

*Whatsoever things are true,*
*Whatsoever things are honest,*
*Whatsoever things are just,*
*Whatsoever things are pure,*
*Whatsoever things are lovely,*
*Whatsoever things are of good report;*
*If there be any virtue, and if there be any*
*    praise, think on these things.*

*Philippians 4:8*

Develop a shining vision of joy. Whether you're up or down, rich or poor, healthy or not, think only of the good. The mother of three, the one suffering with cancer, thought only of the good. The young woman, whose cancer of the breast returned, focused on the good. Frank, the man who wouldn't die, had a great vision of joy. So did 101-year-old Ruth.

Don't be like the industrialist who surrounded himself with bad thoughts, who forced his negativism on everyone crossing his path. Think only of the good. Don't worry about the bad. It'll take care of itself. Your job is to find all the good you can in yourself, in others and in life. The good is there, believe me. If you look, you'll find plenty of good.

A wise man once said that all the world looks yellow to the jaundiced eye. Therefore, remove the hostility from your heart. Replace it with love and joy. Turn your jaundiced eye into a loving and joyful eye, capable of seeing the love and joy that was always there. Use the five virtues to help you develop a vision of unlimited joy.

## Unfinished Business

It's been 10 years since my mother died, but I still remember her last words as if she said them to me yesterday. She had leukemia, a deadly cancer of the blood. For months she endured chemotherapy, enduring constant illness, vomiting, loss of her hair, ugly skin eruptions, plus general and painful emaciation.

I finally took her home. There, in a rented hospital bed with the rails up, watched around the clock by either myself or a nurse, she lay quietly, a ragged skeleton in my mother's once robust body.

Mom rarely spoke during those last weeks: she hadn't the strength. One evening she opened her eyes and slowly lifted her head a little off the pillow. Then she called me in her feeble voice, "Arn. Arn."

I leaned over the bedrails, putting my left ear close to her mouth so I could hear her.

"Arn," she said. "I never told you I loved you."

My arms began to shake. I turned my head away so she wouldn't see the tears in my eyes. "But, Mom, I know that."

"I never told you."

She put her head back down, closed her eyes and never said another word. Two weeks later she died.

I described what had happened to my wife, Hannah, asking why my mother had felt it necessary to say what was so obvious. Hannah wisely answered: "That was unfinished business that had to be taken care of before she could be at peace."

I'm glad my mother's unfinished business was so loving. How many millions of us have unhappy unfinished business eating away at our insides? Unresolved hostility, unforgiven guilt, gnawing doubts?

Have you any unfinished business? Finish it. Finish it now. Finish your business by telling those you love that you love them, those you appreciate that you appreciate them, those you respect of your respect. Finish your business by telling everyone you feel it's necessary to tell, that you immediately and unconditionally forgive them. And be sure to tell yourself while you're at it.

Finish your business by going back out there and trying again, at whatever it is you've failed to persevere at. Finish your business by filling yourself to the brim with enthusiasm, belief, love, forgiveness and perseverance.

**Make your tomorrows great by finishing your business today.**

## Step By Step To Success

*There is no short cut to longevity; to achieve it is the work of a lifetime.*

*James Crichton-Browne*

We've a lot of habits to unlearn, and many new virtues to make our own. For some, like myself, it is a life-long process of learning the good and forgetting the bad. That's all right. The great among us will become virtuous all at once. The rest of us will take it day by day.

Don't tear your hair out if you make a mistake. Baldness is not a cure for error. Acknowledge your mistake, see what lesson you can learn from it and push it aside. Remember your job is to develop an unshakable vision of joy. Don't waste energy looking back at past problems. Your eyes are in front and so is your future. Forgive yourself and move on with enthusiasm, always looking to the goodness that is in you, and forward to the goodness that will be yours.

If you have difficulty adopting all five virtues at once, and sticking to them with enthusiasm, remember that while "goals by the yard are hard, goals by the inch are a cinch".

### Enthusiasm

If you find it hard to become suddenly enthusiastic, take it step by step. Say your affirmation for enthusiasm over and over every day, at least 20 times a day. Repeat it morning, noon and night *enthusiastically*. Walk and talk as if you were full of enthusiasm. Act enthusiastically. Imagine there's a little button in your "E-spot". Every-time you recite your enthusiasm affirmation, everytime you walk, talk or act enthusiastically, imagine a finger pushing the button in your "E-spot" to release a flood of endorphins and other beneficial substances. Make it a point to give away at least one bundle of enthusiasm every day. Bit by bit, you'll adopt the virtue of enthusi-asm as your own. In no time you'll be more enthusiastic about life than you would ever have imagined.

### Belief

If you can't believe wholeheartedly in yourself all at once, that's all right. Don't get down on yourself. Step by step build your self-love. Remember that belief is the eye of your spirit: What you see is what you get. See yourself as a winner. With your mind's eye, see yourself believing enthusiastically in yourself. See yourself saying that you deserve the best life has to offer. Now see yourself seeing it with two eyes in front of your head. Stand in front of a mirror, point your finger at yourself and say, "I believe in you!" Say it with enthusiasm. Look yourself in the eye as you say that over and over, and as you recite your affirmation for belief. Repeat your affirmation for belief at least 20 times a day, all day long. Let your faith in yourself transform you into an iron pillar of belief.

## Love

If you cannot fill yourself with unconditional love all at once, begin by loving yourself, even if only a little in the beginning. Use your affirmation for self-love to rewrite your mental blueprints. Each and every day, write another line of love into your blueprints. The lines of love will begin to add up. Soon they'll cover a whole page, then an entire volume. The more love already written, the easier the next line is to write. With each bit of self-love you add to your life, even if it's only a tiny bit, your Comfort Zone grows, pushing the Tension Zone that much further away. That's why each additional increment is easier to add.

Start loving others at the same time. Look at the list you drew up, the one showing other people's good qualities. Keep that list in front of you at all times, put it into the forefront of your mind. Mentally review the list of love as you receive your affirmation for love over and over, at least 20 times a day. Every day, give at least one person a piece of your love. With love, as well as the other virtues, giving is getting. The more love you give, the more you'll find in your heart.

## Forgiveness

If you can't forgive everyone all at once, forgive one person at a time. Let the first person be you. And if you can't forgive yourself your misdeeds all at once, begin by forgiving yourself for one error you've made. Keep forgiving yourself an error a day until you've wiped out your unnecessary guilt. Say your affirmation for self-forgiveness as many times as possible — at least 20 times a day.

## Perseverance

Finally, if you have difficulty staying the course, take it a step at a time. Do what needs to be done today. Don't worry about tomorrow or next month. Persevere one day at a time. Dare to go on! Repeat your affirmation for perseverance 20 times a day, all day long, to remind yourself that you're giving it ten thousand more tries, if that's what it takes, because you're not going to give in.

Everyday is a new start, a clean slate to write your virtues on. Tell yourself everyday that today is a great new opportunity to be enthusiastic, to fill yourself with belief and love, to forgive and to persevere. Tell yourself that you've got something to do today. You're going to expand your vision of joy by increasing your stores of enthusiasm, belief, love, forgiveness and perseverance.

## Where There Is Joy

> *Lord, make me an instrument of thy peace.*
> *Where there is hatred; let me sow love;*
> *Where there is injury, pardon;*
> *Where there is doubt, faith;*
> *Where there is despair, hope;*
> *Where there is darkness, light;*
> *Where there is sadness, joy.*
>
> *The Prayer of St. Francis of Assisi*

If you have health and joy, you're as rich as anyone can hope to be. I want you to be incredibly wealthy, the richest person in the world.

Look to the places where there is joy. Think of the places where there is joy, all day long. Let your mind dwell only where there is joy. Develop that vision of joy that will make you rich. You deserve the best life has to offer — it's yours for the taking. Don't live in a dreary sleep of disease and distress. Wake Up! Because You're Alive.

*Other Books By* . . .

# HEALTH COMMUNICATIONS, INC.

Enterprise Center
3201 Southwest 15th Street
Deerfield Beach, FL 33442
Phone: 800-851-9100

*ADULT CHILDREN OF ALCOHOLICS*
Janet Woititz
Over a year on The New York Times Best Seller list,this book is the primer
on Adult Children of Alcoholics.
**ISBN 0-932194-15-X**                                                    **$6.95**

*STRUGGLE FOR INTIMACY*
Janet Woititz
Another best seller, this book gives insightful advice on learning to love
more fully.
**ISBN 0-932194-25-7**                                                    **$6.95**

*DAILY AFFIRMATIONS: For Adult Children of Alcoholics*
Rokelle Lerner
These positive affirmations for every day of the year paint a mental picture
of your life as you choose it to be.
**ISBN 0-932194-27-3**                                                    **$6.95**

*CHOICEMAKING: For Co-dependents, Adult Children and Spirituality
Seekers* — Sharon Wegscheider-Cruse
This useful book defines the problems and solves them in a positive way.
**ISBN 0-932194-26-5**                                                    **$9.95**

*LEARNING TO LOVE YOURSELF: Finding Your Self-Worth*
Sharon Wegscheider-Cruse
"Self-worth is a choice, not a birthright", says the author as she shows us
how we can choose positive self-esteem.
**ISBN 0-932194-39-7**                                                    **$7.95**

*LET GO AND GROW: Recovery for Adult Children*
Robert Ackerman
An in-depth study of the different characteristics of adult children of
alcoholics with guidelines for recovery.
**ISBN 0-932194-51-6**                                                    **$8.95**

*LOST IN THE SHUFFLE: The Co-dependent Reality*
Robert Subby
A look at the unreal rules the co-dependent lives by and the way out of the
dis-eased reality.
**ISBN 0-932194-45-1**                                                    **$8.95**

# New Books . . .
## from Health Communications

*BRADSHAW ON: THE FAMILY: A Revolutionary Way of Self-Discovery*
John Bradshaw
The host of the nationally televised series of the same name shows us how families can be healed and we as individuals can realize our full potential.
**ISBN 0-932194-54-0**                                   **$9.95**

*HEALING THE CHILD WITHIN: Discovery and recovery for Adult Children of Dysfunctional Families* — Charles Whitfield
Dr. Whitfield defines, describes and discovers how we can reach our Child Within to heal and nurture our woundedness.
**ISBN 0-932194-40-0**                                   **$8.95**

*WHISKY'S SONG: An Explicit Story of Surviving in an Alcoholic Home*
Mitzi Chandler
A beautiful but brutal story of growing up where violence and neglect are everyday occurrences conveys a positive message of survival and love.
**ISBN 0-932194-42-7**                                   **$6.95**

# New Books on Spiritual Recovery . . .
## from Health Communications

*THE JOURNEY WITHIN: A Spiritual Path to Recovery*
Ruth Fishel
This book will lead you from your dysfunctional beginnings to the place within where renewal occurs.
**ISBN 0-932194-41-9**                                   **$8.95**

*LEARNING TO LIVE IN THE NOW: 6-Week Personal Plan To Recovery*
Ruth Fishel
The author gently introduces you to the valuable healing tools of meditation, positive creative visualization and affirmations.
**ISBN 0-932194-62-1**                                   **$7.95**

*GENESIS: Spirituality in Recovery for Co-dependents*
by Julie D. Bowden and Herbert L. Gravitz
A self-help spiritual program for adult children of trauma, an in-depth look at "turning it over" and "letting go".
**ISBN 0-932194-56-7**                                   **$6.95**

*GIFTS FOR PERSONAL GROWTH AND RECOVERY*
Wayne Kritsberg
Gifts for healing which include journal writing, breathing, positioning and meditation.
**ISBN 0-932194-60-5**                                   **$6.95**

# Books from . . .
# Health Communications

*THIRTY-TWO ELEPHANT REMINDERS: A Book of Healthy Rules*
Mary M. McKee
Concise advice by 32 wise elephants whose wit and good humor will also
be appearing in a 12-step calendar and greeting cards.
ISBN 0-932194-59-1                                                    $3.95


*BREAKING THE CYCLE OF ADDICTION: For Adult Children of Alcoholics*
Patricia O'Gorman and Philip Oliver-Diaz
For parents who were raised in addicted families, this guide teaches you
about Breaking the Cycle of Addiction from *your* parents to your children.
Must reading for any parent.
ISBN 0-932194-37-0                                                    $8.95


*AFTER THE TEARS: Reclaiming The Personal Losses of Childhood*
Jane Middelton-Moz and Lorie Dwinnel
Your lost childhood must be grieved in order for you to recapture your
self-worth and enjoyment of life. This book will show you how.
ISBN 0-932194-36-2                                                    $7.95


*ADULT CHILDREN OF ALCOHOLICS SYNDROME: From Discovery to Recovery*
Wayne Kritsberg
Through the Family Integration System and foundations for healing the
wounds of an alcoholic-influenced childhood are laid in this important
book.
ISBN 0-932194-30-3                                                    $7.95


*OTHERWISE PERFECT: People and Their Problems with Weight*
Mary S. Stuart and Lynnzy Orr
This book deals with all the varieties of eating disorders, from anorexia to
obesity, and how to cope sensibly and successfully.
ISBN 0-932194-57-5                                                    $7.95

----------------------------------------------------------------

Orders must be prepaid by check, money order, MasterCard or Visa.
Purchase orders from agencies accepted (attach P.O. documentation)
for billing. Net 30 days.

Minimum shipping/handling — $1.25 for orders less than $25. For
orders over $25, add 5% of total for shipping and handling. Florida
residents add 5% sales tax.